A·L·B·E·R·T·A
WILDLIFE
viewing guide

LONE
PINE

Alberta
FORESTRY, LANDS
AND WILDLIFE
Fish and Wildlife

RECREATION, PARKS
AND WILDLIFE FOUNDATION

The Publisher:
Lone Pine Publishing
#206 10426-81 Avenue
Edmonton, Alberta, Canada T6E 1X5

Canadian Cataloguing in Publication Data

Main entry under title:
  Alberta wildlife viewing guide
  ISBN 0-919433-79-0 (bound). — ISBN 0-919433-78-2 (pbk.)

  1. Wildlife watching - Alberta.
QL60.A42 1990 591.97123 C90-091163-8

Front cover photo: Great blue heron by
  Terry Willis/The Mach 2 Stock Exchange Ltd.
Back cover photos: Swallowtail butterfly by M. Bailey,
  Wildlife viewers by Public Lands Division,
  Porcupine by B. Wolitski,
  Polyporus versicolor by C. Wershler
Cover and book design: Yuet Chan
Black and white illustration: Rose-Ann Tisserand and Greg Huculak
  (except the following pages: 17, 20, 42, 43, 54, 56, 69 and 79)
Mapping: Rick Checkland
Printing: Quality Color Press Inc., Edmonton, Alberta, Canada

Contents

Acknowledgements 4

Preface 5

Introduction 7

Key to Symbols... 8

Positive Wildlife Viewing 9

Photographing Wildlife 10

Wildlife Viewing Sites

Region   1:   EDMONTON - Parkland 13

Region   2:   RED DEER - Parkland/Prairie 21

Region   3:   CALGARY - Grassland/River 30

Region   4:   LETHBRIDGE - Mountain/Prairie.............. 39

Region   5:   MEDICINE HAT - Grassland/Water.......... 48

Region   6:   NORTHEAST - Lakeland/Boreal................ 57

Region   7:   NORTHWEST - Parkland/Boreal 68

Region   8:   JASPER/BANFF - Mountains/Foothills 75

Banff Townsite Area 84

Kilometre Guide: Banff to Saskatchewan Crossing 84

Kilometre Guide: Saskatchewan Crossing to Jasper 86

Jasper Townsite Area 87

Kilometre Guide: Edmonton to Calgary 88

Fifty Most Sought after Wildlife Species 91

Directory.. 93

Index 95

Acknowledgements

The production of this book is the result of a cooperative, joint venture effort involving Alberta Forestry, Lands and Wildlife, Lone Pine Publishing, the Recreation, Parks and Wildlife Foundation, Alberta Tourism, Alberta Recreation and Parks, the Canadian Parks Service and the Federation of Alberta Naturalists.

Project management was coordinated by Grant Kennedy of Lone Pine Publishing and Harry Stelfox of Alberta Forestry, Lands and Wildlife. A project steering committee comprised of Peter Lee, Ken Lowe, Don Meredith, Wayne Nordstrom, Lee Anne Palutke, Brian Payne and John Rintoul helped to coordinate agency input to the project.

Major participants associated with Lone Pine's efforts included Yuet Chan, Beata Kurpinski, Phillip Kennedy, Mary Walters Riskin and Jane Spalding of Lone Pine Publishing, and Elaine Butler, Jim Butler, John Dodd, Gail Helgason, and Rob Stewart. Karen McClellan was the Lone Pine project supervisor.

Contributions to viewing site documentation, review of draft contents of the guide, and other forms of support were made by many of the above noted individuals, as well as the following:

John Aldag	Matt Fairbarns	Jim Lange	Amit Saxena
Ken Allen	Carolyn Fish	Roger Lefrancois	Alf Scott
Derry Armstrong	John Folinsbee	Lyle Lester	Duane Sept
Frank Bishop	Rob Gardner	Chel Macdonald	Carol Smith
Ron Bjorge	Scotty Girvan	Bob McFetridge	Kirby Smith
Scott Blake	Bill Glasgow	Gerald McKeating	Herman Stegehuis
Dan Bodie	Leo Gudmundson	Dave Moore	Terry Thormin
Wes Bradford	Fred Hammer	Gavin More	Dave Tuffiel
Eldon Bruns	Geoff Holroyd	Tony Nette	Robyn Usher
Lu Carbyn	Myles Horne	Dave Perraton	Jacques van Pelt
Dick Clayton	Glen Hvenegaard	John Pitcher	Sara Vickerman
Brian Crawford	Derek Johnson	Donna Pletz	Cliff Wallis
Doug Culbert	Rosemary Jones	Norbert Raffael	Cleve Wershler
Heather Dempsey	Grant Kihn	Bill Richards	Ed Whitelock
Dave Ealey	Ruth Kleinbub	Blair Rippin	Laurel Zuk
Jan Edmonds	Norbert Kondla	Wayne Roberts	Ken Zurfluh
Gary Erickson	Jane Lancaster	Norm Rodseth	Shaun Zwerzinski

Many other individuals, too numerous to mention here, provided helpful advice and support to the project.

Financial sponsors for this viewing guide were Alberta Forestry, Lands and Wildlife (Fish and Wildlife, Land Information Services and Public Lands divisions), the Recreation, Parks and Wildlife Foundation, and Lone Pine Publishing.

Preface

Alberta's landscape is immense and varied, the best of it still wild. An abundance of wildlife species — many only rarely observed elsewhere in North America — has given the province an international reputation as a wildlife viewing area. Alberta offers its residents and visitors unequalled opportunities for the close observation of wildlife which may be otherwise accessible only in books and films.

In the southern grasslands, once rare pronghorn can now be seen grazing in good numbers. Multitudes of breeding waterfowl, including the majestic Canada goose, gather on prairie wetlands, reservoirs and canals. The aspen parkland harbours a variety of hawks and owls, red foxes and coyotes. Scenic meandering rivers, like the Milk, Bow and Red Deer, beckon canoes to thread miles of wooded corridors past white-tailed deer and songbirds. The vast wildland of the northern boreal forest is home to Canada lynx, caribou, owls, and a host of lake dwellers such as river otters, American white pelicans and grebes.

The Rocky Mountain highway corridor connecting Banff and Jasper national parks is one of the world's great scenic wildlife drives, along with Denali in Alaska, Hayden Valley of Yellowstone, and the safari circuits of Amboseli Park in Kenya. Only in the northern wilds of Wood Buffalo, North America's largest national park, do wolves still prey upon bison, and rare whooping cranes still return to nest.

Explore this province. Sit among the shimmering flocks of migrating arctic shorebirds at Beaverhill and Kimiwan lakes. Acquaint yourself with the colourful wood warblers in Sir Winston Churchill Park. Howl in the moonlight for a gray wolf at Jasper. Sleep under the stars and listen to the coyotes and great horned owls at Writing-on-Stone Provincial Park. Search the trail sides in June for rare orchids at Waterton Lakes National Park.

Focus your camera on the face of a great gray owl or bighorn sheep. Let your canoe carry you silently past drinking mule deer. Walk the same trails as the grizzly bear. Listen to the elk bugle, the loon wail, the deafening chorus of great plains toads, or the aerial trills of a singing pipit. Sit silently by a boreal watering hole waiting for crossbills. Along a northern stream, see arctic grayling gracefully rise for floating mayflies.

The range of Alberta's watchable wildlife is beyond imagination. You won't see it all. No one ever has. But that which you discover will share the years with you.

Getting the Most out of Watching Wildlife

While this guidebook may assist you in finding many of Alberta's important wildlife areas, seeking and finding wildlife closely and consistently requires special skill. Choose your viewing times and destinations carefully, by thinking through your intentions. A wildlife experience has three stages: anticipation, participation and recollection. If you cut short the first through little forethought, you decrease a trip's full potential.

Although early mornings are invariably the best times for most wildlife activity, you should explore a range of periods, especially late evening and after dark. Sitting quietly for extensive periods in one place makes good sense at water holes in the grasslands, badlands and even boreal forests, where many birds remain high in the evergreen spires, otherwise defying good observation. Learn to use vegetation and even your car as a blind for wildlife viewing. Use proper binoculars or a spotting scope - they are basic equipment today. Be patient, and allow for more time than you likely have anticipated. Speak with others about what you are searching for, and share your discoveries with those you meet who have similar interests. Worthwhile friendships and reciprocal information will often be the result. Take advantage of available facilities, publications, field guides, and interpretive programs.

When in the field, move slowly and quietly. When in close proximity of wildlife keep your actions especially slow, avoiding quick movements. Brightly coloured or "noisy" clothing will also decrease your chances of seeing shy and elusive species. Use not just your eyes, but also your ears to locate wildlife. If you are searching for particular birds, learn their songs first from one of the many available record or cassette sets. Do not simply list the species you meet, but get to know them, and think about the behaviors you observe. Keep an on-going notebook of the details and circumstances of your observations. You will be glad that you did at some later time.

Relish the discoveries you make, and avoid becoming obsessed with the sightings you missed. Those will wait for another day. Most effective wildlife viewing represents simply good common sense. Fostering proper skills will serve as good example for others and provide for yourself a more meaningful and enjoyable experience.

Jim Butler
Professor, Parks, Wildlife and Interpretation
The University of Alberta

Introduction

Thousands of people travel every year to one or more of Alberta's many natural areas with the express purpose of observing, studying and photographing wildlife.

This guide is for the residents of Alberta, and visitors as well, who share this fascination. It is a book to keep nearby: in the car, in the backpack, in the saddlebag. Use it to choose specific destinations for a day trip or a multiple-day excursion, or to enhance a trip you've undertaken for another purpose. Consult it in your search for specific wildlife species, or as an introduction to the flora and fauna of the various geographic and ecological regions.

The *Alberta Wildlife Viewing Guide* is intended as a starting point. Use it in conjunction with field guides and natural history books to increase your understanding of the species that you encounter. You may see species which are not mentioned here; others, particularly the more elusive ones, may be seen only after hours or even days of patient, quiet waiting. Wildlife symbols in this book highlight the more viewable or distinctive species at each site, and contact numbers have been provided for additional information regarding site facilities, access and interpretive resources. In addition, as part of Alberta's Watchable Wildlife program, selected wildlife viewing sites will be identified by the observation/viewpoint symbol (see p.8) on signs posted along Alberta's major highways.

Begin your discovery of Alberta's watchable wildlife at any of the sixty-one sites included here. The guide presents only a sampling of the abundant and diverse wildlife resources and viewing opportunities to be found throughout the province. Binoculars, a camera, and time for leisurely exploration will soon reveal the enchantments of Alberta's rich wildlife heritage.

A Note to Readers

This is the first *Alberta Wildlife Viewing Guide*. We hope it will be succeeded by larger, more comprehensive editions as the pleasure of wildlife viewing becomes an increasingly significant feature of the lives of both Albertans and their visitors.

We invite recommendations regarding changes and additions for future editions. All aspects of the guide are appropriate to reader review, and the copublishers welcome comments and suggestions. Please write to either:

Fish and Wildlife Division
Alberta Forestry, Lands and Wildlife
Main Flr., 9945-108 St.
Edmonton, Alberta T5K 2G6
Attn: Coordinator,
Alberta's Watchable Wildlife

Lone Pine Publishing
Suite 206
10426-81 Ave.
Edmonton, Alberta
T6E 1X5

Key to Symbols

Wildlife Symbols:

 Songbirds

 Hoofed Mammals

 Upland birds

 Carnivores

 Waterfowl

 Aquatic Mammals

 Shorebirds

 Fish

 Other Water Birds

 Reptiles / Amphibians

 Birds of Prey

 Insects

 Small Mammals

 Wildflowers

Facilities Symbols:

 Brochures / Checklists

 Wheelchair Accessible

 Interpretive Displays

 Hiking / Walking Trail

 Self-guided Trail

 Picnic / Day Use

 Guided Tour

 Tent Camping

 Observation Platform / Viewpoints

 Toilets

Positive Wildlife Viewing

Public interest in wildlife has never been greater. Bird watching alone has attracted nearly thirty million North Americans, and every year more than twenty-two percent of Canadians travel to observe and photograph wildlife.

This interest, however, has had its consequences. Although people are more conscious of preserving wildlife, critical habitats have nevertheless experienced frequent harassment and increasing pressure from humans. Consequently, some wildlife ranges have been reduced, and some species have even been displaced.

Modern wildlife viewing demands courtesy and common sense — including respect for animals and their habitats, knowledge of local regulations, and consideration for private property and the activities of others.

Today's ethics for the field include the following:

- Confine your movements wherever possible to designated trails, viewing platforms and blinds.
- Avoid nesting sites, and respect the resting periods of animals and birds. Never chase or flush wildlife.
- Keep a respectful distance, for the animal's sake — and occasionally for your own.
- Leave viewing sites, including the flora as well as the fauna, undamaged by your visits.

Respect and good judgement by today's wildlife watchers are essential to the preservation of Alberta's natural heritage for future generations.

Jim Butler

Photographing Wildlife

The best photographers learn patience. You may need to sit near a pond for hours to gain the trust of beavers, or stand in a marsh all morning for a shot of a heron in flight.

After an extended period of time, many animals and birds will accept you as part of the surrounding territory and resume their normal activities. By moving — slowly — only when the animal is looking the other way, you can often get close enough to mammals such as mule deer and wapiti for great telephoto shots. Blinds and zoom lenses are helpful, and multi-coloured clothing will help to break up the human form in the animal's eyes.

Getting closer than telephoto range to large mammals or even some of the more aggressive birds is hazardous. Although wapiti look their best during the rutting season in mid-autumn, for example, the bulls can be dangerous at this time. Moose can be aggressive at any time, and shouldn't be approached as closely as other ungulates. Bears should never be approached: use a long lens for them, or use your vehicle as a screen, and remember to compensate for their dark coats by opening up the lens aperture.

Avoid approaching nests too closely: you will not only alarm the birds, but ruin your chances for a stunning photograph. Never attempt to photograph raptors (hawks and owls) while they are laying or incubating eggs as they are very likely to abandon the nest. Stay at a distance, with a tripod and a zoom lens, and wait for the birds to come into your viewing range.

You'll need a long telephoto lens to photograph such elusive species as mountain goats and bald eagles.

Framing and Lighting Your Photographs

The early morning hours (until about 10 a.m.), when birds and animals are most active, can be the best times for photography. The early light defines shape and colour better than the intense light of midday, which flattens contrast and washes out colour.

Avoid distracting backgrounds in your photographs by focusing as closely as possible on the subject, or by reducing the field depth. By opening the lens aperture, the background will blur, leaving your subject to stand out in clear focus.

Shoot on the same level as your subject (or slightly below) whenever possible. A photograph taken from above frequently results in the subject's being lost in the background.

Use a faster shutter speed (1/500th of a second or more) for birds in flight, or for running mammals. Also, the use of a motor drive for a rapid succession of shots will increase chances of getting that perfect picture. Panning the camera with a moving animal while clicking the shutter will create an impression of movement, as the background will blur.

Many of the smaller animals and dozens of varieties of birds and wildflowers are seen most often in low-light situations: in deep forest, just after dawn, or near sunset. High-speed film can produce good results under these circumstances.

Flash equipment may provide sharper, more colourful images on dull days, and may help to eliminate distracting shadows, thereby providing better images of dark-coloured birds and small mammals.

Avoid back-lighting, except for special effects. This can work well with flowers.

Equipment

A **35-mm single lens reflex camera** is most frequently used for wildlife photography, and is all you really need.

Take along an **adequate supply of film**, of varying speeds. It is worthwhile to pack all camera equipment — and film — in waterproof, protective cases.

Tripods are a must for low light situations and when slow shutter speeds are to be used. To obtain high quality, sharply focused photographs, the camera must be perfectly still and this can only be achieved with a tripod.

Appropriate **lenses** and **filters** can improve your photographs. A telephoto lens that can focus down to about 15 feet is almost essential for birds and mammals. Extension tubes can reduce the focus distance even further, thus increasing the image size on the film.

A lens that will focus to nine inches will be needed for recording wildflowers and butterflies. Zoom lenses are particularly convenient, but will reduce the amount of incoming light, which may present problems.

A skylight (UV) filter will cut reflection, intensify colour and help in photographing fish in streams.

Lenses larger than 300 mm usually require a tripod or other support for the camera.

While portable **blinds** are ideal for all wildlife photography, excellent pictures can be obtained from the windows of a parked car, a canoe, or anything else that helps to hide or break up the human shape in the eyes of mammals and birds. Even a piece of burlap draped over the head and upper body can help.

Take along a **notebook** with a waterproof cover and a pencil (which writes more easily than pen on damp paper). In it, you can record the time and location of your shots to assist in organizing your photographs after the trip. You may also find it useful to record lens aperture settings, lenses used, film speed, and so on, in order to more quickly build your wildlife photography expertise.

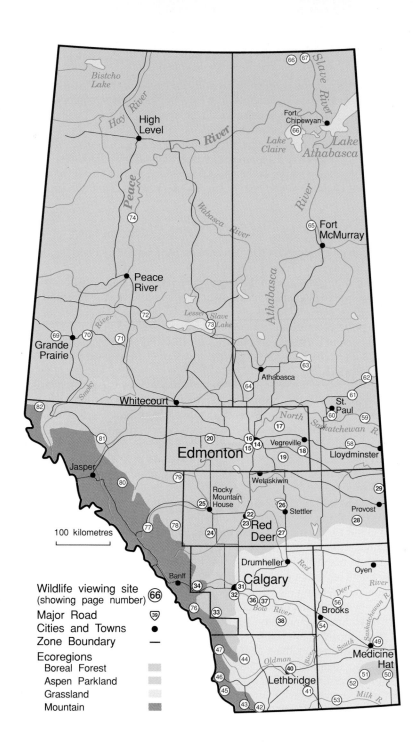

100 kilometres

Wildlife viewing site
(showing page number) ⑥⑥
Major Road ㊴
Cities and Towns ●
Zone Boundary —
Ecoregions
  Boreal Forest
  Aspen Parkland
  Grassland
  Mountain

EDMONTON
Parkland

The viewing sites in this region feature some of the many lakes where small mammals, songbirds and a variety of migrating waterfowl enjoy the shelter and abundant food supplies of the parkland habitat.

The parkland region falls between the dense mixed-wood boreal forest to the north, and the prairie grassland to the south. Aspen and balsam poplar are common here, favouring richer soils where fires have occurred. Moderate precipitation along with variable soils and agricultural land uses create a unique mosaic of tall shrubs, deciduous trees, grassland and farmland.

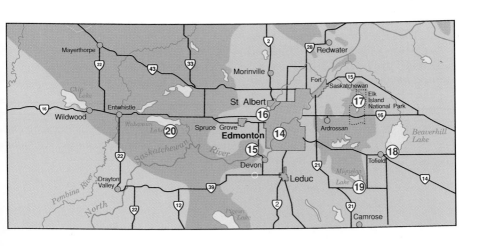

Wildlife Viewing Site (66) (showing page number)	Ecozones
Major Roads (39)	Aspen Parkland
Cities and Towns ○	Boreal Mixedwood
National Park	Boreal Foothills

50 kilometres

Whitemud Creek Ravine

Northern saw-whet owl

Hidden within the deeply incised Whitemud Creek Ravine is a tranquil natural setting surrounded by the bustle of suburban life in southwest Edmonton.

White-tailed and mule deer, snowshoe hares and coyotes thrive in the heavily wooded security of the ravine.

On an early May morning, listen for the raspy honk of cock pheasants, or the loud ratchet drumming of pileated woodpeckers. You might see a merlin making a high speed chase for its prey over the tree tops. In winter, merlins are especially attracted to the large flocks of foraging bohemian waxwings. Other birds drawn to the area are spotted sandpipers, belted kingfishers, northern orioles, ruby-crowned kinglets, and northern saw-whet owls.

The John Janzen Nature Centre, just west of the mouth of Whitemud Creek, provides nature information for all of Edmonton; the centre also stages family events throughout the year.

> Peregrine falcons live on the roof of the AGT building in downtown Edmonton. They can be viewed from a video display in the building which also shows recorded footage; there is a small admission fee of fifty cents.

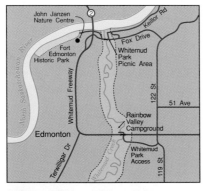

Directions: Access Whitemud Park from Keillor Rd. off Fox Dr. or from 122 St. just south of Whitemud Freeway.

John Janzen Nature Centre, Edmonton 428-7900
Fish and Wildlife Division, Edmonton 427-3574

Clifford E. Lee Nature Sanctuary

Seeing muskrats at close range, Canada geese on flax bales installed as nesting platforms, the courtship of American coots and the flights of broad-winged hawks are among the many wildlife experiences to be enjoyed at this sanctuary. A board-walk and established trails make it an excellent destination for a family outing.

More than a hundred species of birds live in this habitat of marshes, sandhills, meadows, and aspen and pine woods. They include red-necked grebes, American bittern and ruffed grouse.

Spring and fall are the best times to see bird life, but mammals such as snowshoe hares, mule and white-tailed deer, and coyotes can be seen year-round.

From May to August, the sanctuary is bright with wildflowers. Lily-of-the-valley and wintergreen both flower in early June. Yellow lady's-slippers bloom at the edge of meadows in June, while a host of meadow flowers blossom in July. Showy fringed gentians and evening primrose round out the flowering season in July and August.

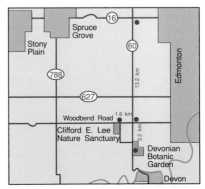

Muskrat

Directions: Take Devon turnoff from Hwy. 16 and go south 13.2 km to Woodbend Rd., turn west for 1.6 km then south 1.4 km to parking pull-off.

Fish and Wildlife Division,
Stony Plain 963-6131
Fish and Wildlife Division,
Edmonton 427-3574

Wagner Natural Area

Approximately one third of all of Alberta's plant species can be found in this area of black spruce forests, willow-sedge fens, mixed-wood forests and calcium-rich ponds. The fifteen different species of orchids include the more common northern green bog, sparrow's egg and lady's-slipper, as well as rare species, like the bog adder's-mouth orchid.

On the 1.2 kilometre self-guiding trail and board-walk through the forests and fens, look for unusual carnivorous plants such as the sundew, bladder-wort and butterwort.

A total of 138 bird species have been recorded at Wagner, 97 of which are known to have nested here. Least flycatchers, yellow-rumped warblers and dark-eyed juncos are common, as are typically boreal species such as the ruby-crowned kinglet and boreal chickadee. Pileated woodpeckers and northern gos-hawks frequent the mature woodlands, and the calls of northern saw-whet and great horned owls may be heard at dusk.

The ponds are home to wood frogs, boreal chorus frogs, and western toads. "Toading walks" are conducted in the spring.

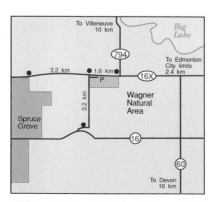

Least flycatcher and nest

ALL BY C. WERSHLER

Boreal chorus frog

To Villeneuve
10 km

Big Lake

794

To Edmonton
City limits
2.4 km

3.2 km   1.6 km

16X

P

Wagner
Natural
Area

3.2 km

Spruce
Grove

16

60

To Devon
16 km

Public Lands Division,
Sherwood Park 464-7955
Public Lands Division,
Edmonton 427-5209

Elk Island National Park

An extraordinarily high density of animals makes Elk Island one of the best places in Alberta for year-round wildlife watching. More than one hundred kilometres of trails for hiking and skiing extend throughout this fenced wilderness of lakes, spruce bogs, low forested hills and meadows. Five hundred plains bison, 400 wood bison, 400 moose and 1600 wapiti range throughout the park. Coyotes are often seen along the roadside. The park is also home to over 2000

Plains bison

beavers. In the transitional aspen forest, 228 bird species have been recorded, including red-eyed vireos, least flycatchers, song sparrows, northern saw-whet and great horned owls.

At Astotin Lake, the interpretive Lakeview Trail and Living Waters boardwalk follow the water's edge, where you may glimpse double-crested cormorants, great blue herons, and black-crowned night herons. In summer, the red-necked grebe with its loud, wailing call is the most prominent waterfowl bird to be seen. The lake is one of the few places outside the mountains where Barrow's goldeneyes nest.

Red-necked grebe

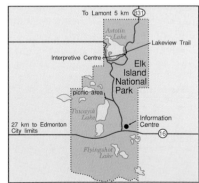

Canadian Parks Service,
Park Office 992-6380
Fish and Wildlife Division,
Edmonton 427-3574

Beaverhill Natural Area

C. WERSHLER

Snow geese

D. GRIFFIN

Beaverhill Lake is nationally and internationally recognized for waterfowl migration and observation. More than 253 species of birds have been reported here.

In March, Canada geese arrive by the thousands, followed by white-fronted geese, snow geese, tundra swans and numerous duck species. Birds of prey soon arrive: rough-legged and red-tailed hawks, bald eagles, merlins, northern harriers, northern goshawks and peregrine falcons. The southern end of Beaverhill Lake is famous for its shorebird numbers, where more than forty species have been reported. As a result of the hundreds of nest boxes placed here for their use, the area also supports the largest concentration of nesting tree swallows in Alberta.

The Beaverhill Bird Observatory, located at the southeast corner of the lake, offers instructional tours in spring and summer. From the parking area, a trail winds past marsh wetlands and a viewing mound, and towards Beaverhill Lake.

Beaverhill Lake Nature Centre, just outside of Tofield, provides further information on wildlife found in the area.

Beaverhill Lake Nature Centre, Tofield, 662-3191; Public Lands Div., Sherwood Park 464-7955

EDMONTON PARKLAND

Miquelon Lake Provincial Park

The aspen-balsam poplar woodland of this area represents the northern portion of the aspen parkland belt. This vegetation type has been cleared or seriously disturbed in many places, and it is increasingly difficult to find undisturbed areas outside of the Cooking Lake Moraine — which includes this park.

Wild roses, saskatoons, wild raspberries, buffaloberries, pincherries and dogwood cover the woodland area.

Songbirds abound, especially species characteristic of older woodland such as western wood pewees, ovenbirds, yellow warblers, northern orioles and rose-breasted grosbeaks.

Aspen-fringed ponds attracts ducks and grebes. Freshwater marsh areas are inhabited by sora, and occasionally visited by green-winged teals, American coots and ruddy ducks. California and ring-billed gulls nest in large numbers on Gull Island.

Plains and red-sided garter snakes are common, and in the spring, wood and boreal chorus frogs call from the ponds.

Look for moose and white-tailed and mule deer in the early morning or evening.

The adjacent wildlife sanctuary offers many kilometres of hiking trails.

Saskatoon berries

Plains garter snake

Provincial Parks Service,
Park Office 672-7308
Fish and Wildlife Division, Camrose 679-1225

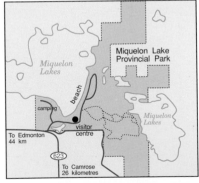

Wabamun Lake

Winter provides a unique opportunity for waterfowl viewing in this area, as the power plants at Wabamun, Sundance and Keephills provide year-round open water for hooded mergansers, bald eagles, and several thousand mallards.

Red-winged blackbird

A large variety of migrating, breeding and moulting waterbirds can be seen here, including gulls, terns, rails, herons, loons, kingfishers, sandpipers, and even American white pelicans. Ospreys nest at both Wabamun Lake and nearby Lake Isle, and there are nesting colonies of red-necked and western grebes. This transition zone, a combination of rolling moraine, parkland, mixed-wood forest, bog and sandy pine areas, supports birds such as common ravens, gray jays and great gray owls, which are normally expected further to the north and west.

Beaver

J. BUTLER

Beavers and muskrats use the lake while the surrounding upland is home to coyotes, porcupines, moose and white-tailed deer. The lake contains northern pike, lake whitefish, yellow perch and walleye. Whitefish can be seen spawning in the shallows by the railway trestle during October and November.

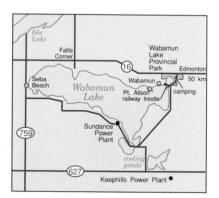

Provincial Parks Service,
Wabamun Lake Provincial Park, 892-2711
Fish and Wildlife Division,
Stony Plain 963-6131

20

RED DEER
Parkland / Prairie

This area, rich in lakes, provides excellent opportunities for viewing aquatic mammals, fish, waterfowl and shorebirds. The many species of migrant birds which visit here in spring and fall are of particular interest.

A transition zone from moist aspen parkland to dry prairie, this area offers a distinct blend of habitats for wildlife. Wildflowers flourish on the open hillsides, while localized aspen stands and shrub thickets provide shelter for deer, foxes, coyotes and many smaller mammals.

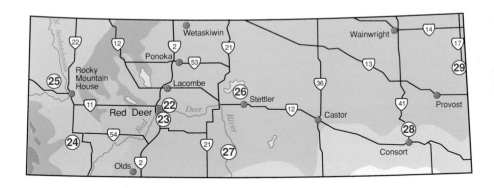

Wildlife Viewing Site 66
(showing page number)

Major Roads -39-

Cities and Towns ●

50 kilometres

Ecozones
Short grass
Mixed grass
Aspen parkland
Boreal mixedwood
Boreal foothills
Boreal uplands
Subalpine

Gaetz Lake Sanctuary

Two oxbow lakes provide the centre of attraction in this outstanding urban wildlife reserve. Fed by springs, the streams and wetlands nurture rare orchids and many other wildflowers. These include lily-of-the-valley, blue clematis and fairy bells in the spring, and evening primrose, Bicknell's geranium and yellow lady's-slipper in the summer.

Yellow lady's-slipper

Yellow-headed and red-winged blackbirds are prominent in the willow and cattail margins of the lake. The surrounding mixed woodland and old growth forest provide habitat for pileated and three-toed woodpeckers, black-capped and boreal chickadees, red-breasted nuthatches, white-throated sparrows and olive-sided flycatchers.

Take advantage of the viewing blinds and platforms to see grebes, coots and ducks, which all nest at the sanctuary. One can also view Canada geese regularly.

Muskrats and beavers are year-round inhabitants; coyotes, red foxes, white-tailed and mule deer are seen frequently in the winter.

The Kerry Wood Nature Centre here offers nature walks, exhibits, an excellent selection of books, and a bulletin board featuring recent wildlife sightings.

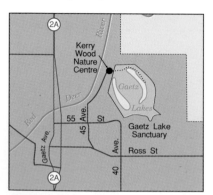

Downy woodpecker

Directions: Turn east from Gaetz Ave. onto 55 St., then north on 45 Ave. for 1.2 km.

Kerry Wood Nature Centre,
Red Deer 346-2010
Fish and Wildlife Division,
Red Deer 340-5142

RED DEER   PARKLAND / PRAIRIE

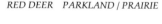

Slack Slough

Slack Slough

This extensive bulrush marsh is an exceptional area for viewing water-fowl—including a variety of diving and dabbling ducks—and a diversity of marsh birds. Good viewing opportunities with binoculars or a spotting scope are available at the raised viewing platform on the north side of the slough. Preservation of permanent, marshy water bodies of this kind in the aspen parkland is extremely important for maintaining waterfowl populations.

Canada geese, common goldeneyes and buffleheads are common in spring and summer. Tundra swans frequent the area during migration. Mallards and eared grebes are abundant. Birds of prey such as northern harriers and red-tailed hawks may also be seen.

The area is replete with wildflowers, including purple and white violets, shooting stars, Canada anemone and purple milk vetch.

Shooting star

Fish and Wildlife Division,
Red Deer 340-5142

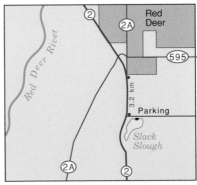

Burnstick Lake

Extensive areas of bulrushes and water-lilies make this a scenic spot for canoeing. Common loons nest here, as do grebes and ducks. Pike and perch can be seen, and aquatic mammals such as beaver, muskrat and mink are common.

Much of the shoreline is mixed-wood forest, where hikers can observe mule deer, moose, ruffed grouse and spruce grouse.

A nearby point of interest is Birch Lake, located 1.6 kilometres to the north and accessible by gravelled

Great blue heron

Ruffed grouse

oil-well roads. Here, northern orioles can be seen nesting in the mature poplars around the shore, and the area supports a great blue heron rookery as well. The nest trees of the herons can be observed from the northeast access point without disturbing the adult birds, by using binoculars or a spotting scope.

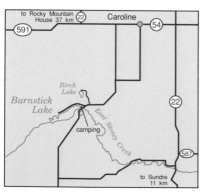

Fish and Wildlife Division,
Rocky Mountain House 845-8230
Alberta Forest Service,
Sundre 638-3805

Crimson Lake Provincial Park

Hiking trails wind through black spruce bogs, tamarack swamps, open sedge and shrub fens and the typical foothills vegetation of lodgepole pine and aspen. Vegetated sand dunes add to the diversity of the flora.

Crimson Lake Provincial Park is a good place to view wildflowers, including up to thirteen orchid species, buckbean and two varieties of sundew. The latter

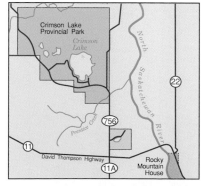

*Crimson Lake (above);
Calypso orchid (top)*

C. WERSHLER (ABOVE)

use their sticky hairs to trap insects for food. Other wet-area plants include marsh cinquefoils, colt's-foot and marsh marigolds.

The park supports populations of sandhill cranes, boreal owls, northern pygmy-owls, greater yellowlegs, western tanagers and solitary sandpipers. Mammals include northern bog lemmings and water and pygmy shrews.

Provincial Parks Service,
Park Office 845-2340
Fish and Wildlife Division,
Rocky Mountain House 845-8230

25

Buffalo Lake

Buffalo Lake is surrounded by rolling hills, part of the "knob and kettle" landscape left by retreating glaciers. The large lake with its many shallow bays provides nesting sites for great blue herons, black-crowned night-herons, plenty of Canada geese and ducks as well as common terns, American avocets and ring-billed gulls. Ross' geese, American white pelicans and piping plovers have also been seen.

The parkland woods are inhabited by white-tailed deer, mule deer, coyotes and ruffed grouse. Colourful northern orioles nest in the tops of the tall trembling aspens, and the descending call of the western wood-pewee is commonly heard. Raptors include great horned owls, short-eared owls, golden and bald eagles as well as many of the hawk species found in Alberta.

Rochon Sands Provincial Park on the southeast side of the lake offers good camping facilities and the best access to the lake.

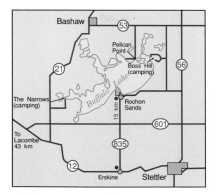

M. PYBUS

White-tailed deer and fawn

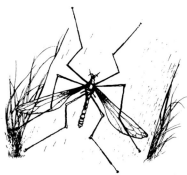

Crane fly

Provincial Parks Service,
Rochon Sands Provincial Park 742-4338
Fish and Wildlife Division,
Stettler 742-7510

Dry Island Buffalo Jump Provincial Park

More than 150 bird species have been spotted in this provincial park, including turkey vultures, golden eagles, red-tailed and Swainson's hawks, prairie falcons, mountain bluebirds, belted kingfishers and several kinds of warblers. The shady riverbanks and exposed river flats are good places to view ducks and wading birds such as great blue herons, marbled godwits and willets.

Dry Island Buffalo Jump

Beavers and muskrats live by the river. In upland areas, white-tailed and mule deer, coyotes, white-tailed jackrabbits and badgers are often seen.

In late July and early August the Red Deer River becomes the setting for a dramatic natural spectacle, when goldeye come to the surface in great numbers to feed on clouds of newly hatched white mayflies. For the best view of this phenomenon, approach the water at dusk and illuminate the surface of the river with a flashlight beam.

Park facilities are open from May 1 to October 31.

Cliff swallow nests

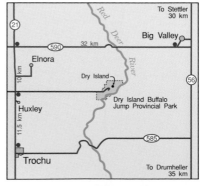

Provincial Parks Service,
Park Office 442-4211
Provincial Parks Service,
Midland Provincial Park 823-4788

Gooseberry Lake Provincial Park

Aspen woods

Prickly rose

Gooseberry Lake is a high alkaline body of water, fed by seepage springs which sustain a variety of interesting plants. In the upland areas aspen, balsam-poplar woods and shrub thickets create a rich environment for wildlife.

This is a major staging area for migrating shorebirds. Thousands of red-necked phalaropes may be seen on the lake each May and August. Gooseberry Lake is also a late summer staging area for ducks, geese and swans. Other water birds — gulls, great blue herons, and American white pelicans — and shorebirds such as lesser yellowlegs are common in this area.

The park's woods accommodate both small and large mammals. Look for deer mice, red squirrels, chipmunks, snowshoe hares and thirteen-lined ground squirrels. White-tailed and mule deer are common here.

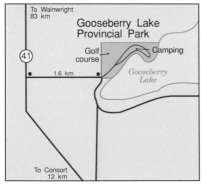

To Wainwright
83 km

Gooseberry Lake
Provincial Park

(41)   Golf
       course   Camping

1.6 km   *Gooseberry
                Lake*

To Consort
12 km

Provincial Parks Service,
Park Office 577-2241
Provincial Parks Service,
Vermilion Provincial Park 853-8159

Dillberry Lake Provincial Park

Thirteen-lined ground squirrel

Western wood lily

Stunted aspen growing on sand dunes combine with scattered lakes, grasslands and shrubland to create this intriguing landscape.

The sandy aspen parkland contains an unusual mix of boreal forest species like the hermit thrush, grassland species such as the lark sparrow, along with the more typical aspen parkland species. Look for marsh wrens, yellow-headed blackbirds, western meadowlarks and Sprague's pipits.

Ducks, geese and swans are common on the waters of Dillberry Lake, and shorebirds and herons frequent its shores.

Thirteen-lined ground squirrels are typical inhabitants of this parkland, where dry sandy soils stunt the growth of trees and shrubs. Wildflowers abound, particularly brown-eyed Susans, crocuses, asters and western wood lilies.

Provincial Parks Service,
Park Office 858-3824
Fish and Wildlife Division,
Lloydminster 871-6495

To Chauvin
18 km

17

Alberta
Saskatchewan

Dillberry Lake
Provincial Park

camping

Killarney
Lake

Dillberry Lake

Leane
Lake

CALGARY
Grassland / River

Although much of the grassland is now devoted to ranching and urban development, protected areas — both within the city and outside it — are havens for the naturalist.

In this region, the prairie grasses grow taller than in the more arid prairie to the south and east. Here, hawks and eagles soar above the hills, cacti flower on the uplands, and bighorn sheep gather against river canyon walls. Along the many creeks and rivers, beavers, muskrats and a variety of birds thrive in dense mixed-wood and poplar forests.

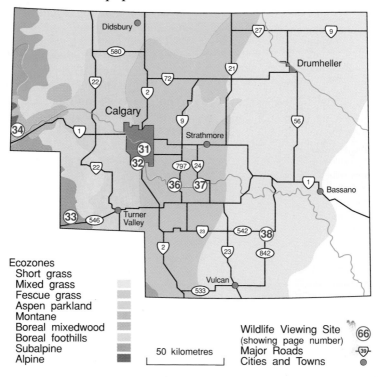

Ecozones
  Short grass
  Mixed grass
  Fescue grass
  Aspen parkland
  Montane
  Boreal mixedwood
  Boreal foothills
  Subalpine
  Alpine

50 kilometres

Wildlife Viewing Site (66)
(showing page number)
Major Roads (39)
Cities and Towns ●

Inglewood Bird Sanctuary

Three kilometres of peaceful nature trails lead past floodplain ponds and along the Bow River through grassland, shrubs and riverbank cottonwoods. Two hundred and sixteen bird species and 271 plant species have been recorded here. Prominent birds include bald eagles, Swainson's hawks, nesting great horned owls, ring-necked pheasants, gray partridges and a range of warbler species.

The backwaters and old channels have been protected as a chain of lagoons that provide nesting sites for many ducks and Canada geese. This is likely the best place in the province for seeing wood ducks. Mallards, common goldeneyes and common mergansers live here year-round, along with

Great horned owl

muskrats and beavers. The sanctuary, only a few kilometres from the city centre, is also home to white-tailed and mule deer, coyotes, foxes and long-tailed weasels.

This is a lovely spot for morning or evening nature walks, and a welcome escape from the bustle of the city during lunch hour.

Look for the peregrine falcons which nest atop the AGT building in downtown Calgary. They can be observed from through television monitors at the AGT building and the Calgary Zoo; there are interpretive programs at both sites.

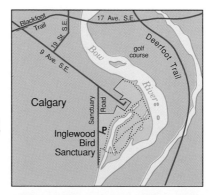

Directions: From the south access 9 Ave. SE from Macleod Tr. or Blackfoot Tr. and go east to Sanctuary Road. From the north access from Deerfoot Tr. via 17 Ave. and turn south on 19 St. to 9 Ave.

Calgary Parks and Recreation, 269-6688
Fish and Wildlife Division,
Calgary 297-6423

Fish Creek Provincial Park

Fish Creek

This urban park is an island of natural habitat located along the southern edge of Calgary. A visitor centre offers year-round events and interpretive displays. Beside the centre is Bow Valley Ranch, a collection of historic buildings dating from 1896.

Over 180 species of birds have been sighted at the park. Great blue herons are common along the watercourses, ducks and geese can be seen on the Bow River year-round, and bald eagles soar along the valley in winter. Red-tailed hawks, Swainson's hawks and great horned owls are raptors common to the area.

White-tailed and mule deer are seen in early morning and late evening, and coyotes and badgers may be spotted patrolling the grasslands.

West of Macleod Trail the Fish Creek valley is much narrower and steeper. Notice the beaver ponds along Fish Creek. Dense spruce and aspen forest provide excellent habitat for songbirds.

Badger

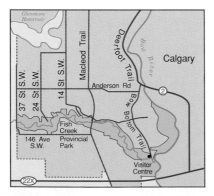

Provincial Parks Service,
Parks Office 297-5293
Fish and Wildlife Division,
Calgary 297-6423

CALGARY   GRASSLAND / RIVER

Sheep River Wildlife Sanctuary

Sheep River Wildlife Sanctuary   *Bighorn sheep*

A large band of bighorn sheep lives year-round in this sanctuary, with its abundant grasslands and convenient escape routes along the river canyon walls. The sanctuary is an excellent place to watch sheep feeding, interacting and on occasion, being stalked by coyotes. During the fall, mature rams can often be closely observed from the comfort of your vehicle.

This is one of the best areas in the province for observing migrating birds of prey which follow the foothill ridges in spring and fall. Nearly all of Alberta's birds of prey have been recorded here during migration, and golden eagles are especially prominent.

Cougars, secretive animals which move primarily at night, have occasionally been observed in the area. Look for Columbian ground squirrels on the grassland slopes in the summer. Further west near Bluerock Campground, American dippers and an occasional harlequin duck can be found along the fast-flowing river.

The sanctuary is closed to vehicles Dec. 1 to May 15 to protect the winter sheep range.

Fish and Wildlife Division,
Calgary 297-6423
Alberta Forest Service,
Turner Valley 933-4381

Bow Valley / Yamnuska Mountain

Yamnuska Mountain

Tiger salamander

Yamnuska Mountain rises abruptly from Morley Flats and the Bow River Valley, marking the beginning of the Front Ranges. Hiking trails at the base of the mountain lead past beaver ponds, open meadows, swamps, delicate spring-fed (calcareous) areas, forests of aspen, white spruce and lodgepole pine, and many species of plants; some of which are rare. Orchids are a specialty here — yellow lady's-slippers are especially plentiful — and western wood lilies can also be seen. On other trails leading higher up the mountain, you may spot bighorn sheep or mountain goats.

At both Bow Valley Provincial Park and Yamnuska, look for calliope and rufous hummingbirds and a large variety of songbirds. Three species of chickadee are found in this area and woodpeckers include northern flickers and both species of three-toed woodpeckers. Amphibians include long-toed salamanders, tiger salamanders, boreal toads, wood frogs and spotted frogs.

Prairie falcon (facing page)
D. MOORE

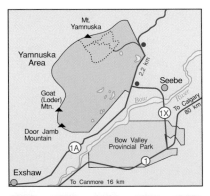

Provincial Parks Service,
Bow Valley Provincial Park 673-3663
Public Lands Division,
Calgary 297-6426

CALGARY   GRASSLAND / RIVER

McKinnon Flats

Great blue herons, eastern kingbirds, northern orioles, mourning doves and tree swallows are commonly seen at this site on the Bow River. The flats provide a varied habitat of willow margins, tall cottonwoods and brushy slopes for an impressive spectrum of songbirds. Water birds include American white pelicans, Canada geese and many duck species. Here, public access is provided to the Bow River and its world class populations of brown trout.

Along the crest of the river valley, birds of prey such as prairie falcons and red-tailed hawks can often be seen patrolling the hillsides for small birds and mammals. Golden eagles and rough-legged hawks may be seen during migration. Bald eagles are reported most winters.

Mule deer browse the bottom land of the river valley and adjacent ravines, and coyotes are present in the area throughout the year.

Polyphemus moth

Mallard

BOTH BY C. WERSHLER

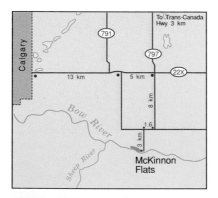

Fish and Wildlife Division,
Calgary 297-6423
Fish and Wildlife Division,
Strathmore 934-3422

Wyndham-Carseland Provincial Park

Lush growth along the river valley of the Bow has created excellent habitats for nesting songbirds. Tall balsam poplars and cottonwoods harbour nests of mourning doves, brown thrashers, eastern kingbirds and tree swallows. Six species of sparrow can be found in open areas or along the hillside. To the west, at the Carseland Dam, you can easily observe a number of fish-eating birds, including belted kingfishers, great blue herons and American white pelicans.

In summer, ferruginous, red-tailed and Swainson's hawks are seen along the slopes of the valley. Bald and golden eagles soar over the dam and river valley during spring and fall migrations.

On the riverbanks you may have the opportunity to observe such aquatic mammals as the beaver and the muskrat. From the park's hiking trails you may also see white-tailed and mule deer.

Brown thrasher

Belted kingfisher

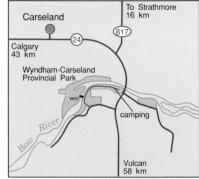

Provincial Parks Service,
Park Office 934-3523
Fish and Wildlife Division,
Strathmore 934-3422

McGregor Lake

American white pelicans and double-crested cormorants often forage on this large prairie reservoir from April to September. In spring and fall, the lake is an important staging area for waterfowl, including snow geese, Canada geese and greater white-fronted geese. Blue-winged teals and northern shovelers can be seen in spring and summer.

American white pelican

The surrounding dry prairie uplands offer opportunities to observe marbled godwits and long-billed curlews. Prairie plants include such exotic species as the cushion cactus with its burgundy blooms and the prickly pear cactus with its prominent yellow blossoms: both flower in June.

Cushion cactus

Spawning lake whitefish can be seen in October at the sluice gate on the northwest corner of the lake. A government campground, picnic area and boat launch are provided at the north end of the lake.

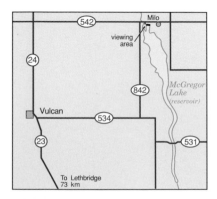

Fish and Wildlife Division,
Lethbridge 381-5283
Fish and Wildlife Division,
Vulcan 485-6971

LETHBRIDGE
Mountain / Prairie

Coulees, prairie, foothills, mountain slopes: the remarkable variety of landforms and climatic conditions in this region produce an exceptional diversity of sites for viewing wildlife.

Coulees are steeply eroded draws and valleys which harbour sufficient moisture to create distinctive oases of trees and shrubbery in the midst of the southern prairie. These locations sustain an abundance of flora, birds and mammals which are otherwise uncommon in the prairie region. In the Crowsnest Pass to the west, you may visit open stands of limber pines, bent and weathered by the wind, fast-flowing trout streams and mountain meadows. The greatest diversity of wildlife species in the province occurs in Alberta's southwest corner, where prairie and mountain meet in Waterton Lakes National Park.

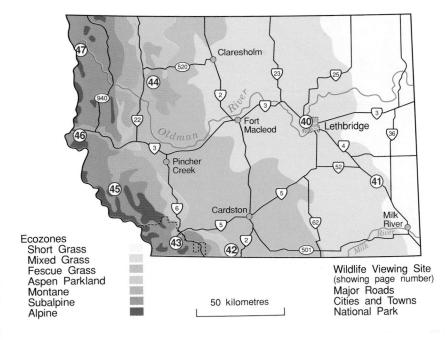

Ecozones
  Short Grass
  Mixed Grass
  Fescue Grass
  Aspen Parkland
  Montane
  Subalpine
  Alpine

50 kilometres

Wildlife Viewing Site
(showing page number) 66
Major Roads
Cities and Towns
National Park

Helen Schuler Coulee Centre

B. WOLITSKI

Porcupine

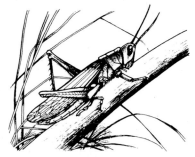

Grasshopper (Melanoplus)

Patches of prickly pear cactus and butte primrose flower amidst the dry grasses of the coulee slopes at the Helen Schuler Coulee Centre in Lethbridge. This area along the Oldman River supports a variety of micro-environments — from shady cottonwoods to dense shrubbery — and attracts a variety of wildlife.

Watch for white-tailed deer, Nuttall's cottontails and porcupines. You may also see great horned owls and northern flickers. Small rodents such as deer mice, meadow voles and northern pocket gophers are found in the river valley. At the nearby Elizabeth Hall Wetlands, keep an eye out for painted turtles.

The Helen Schuler Coulee Centre offers interpretive programs, nature walks, and exhibits on seasonal themes. A system of well-signed nature trails leads away from the centre.

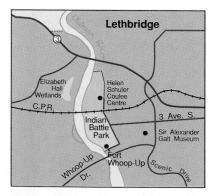

Directions: Access from Scenic Dr. N, then turn west on 3rd. Ave. S.

Helen Schuler Coulee Centre,
Lethbridge 320-3064
Fish and Wildlife Division,
Lethbridge 381-5283

Tyrrell/Rush Lakes

Tyrrell Lake is well known for its trout, and a fisheries access point is situated on the northwest corner of the 384-hectare lake. The adjacent 160 hectares of marsh, including Rush Lake, constitute a staging area for waterfowl, particularly snow geese and tundra swans. Yellow-headed blackbirds, red-winged blackbirds and black-crowned night-herons nest here. In the winter, the marshes provide cover for gray partridges, ring-necked pheasants and white-tailed deer.

Gray partridge chick

Habitat development has increased waterfowl and shorebird populations at this site. American avocets, common snipe, Canada geese, northern pintails, canvasbacks, California and ring-billed gulls and double-crested cormorants are frequently observed in this wetland complex.

Canada geese

Trout may be seen rising to take insects from the surface of lakes, ponds and streams throughout Alberta, particularly in late afternoon and evening during the summer.

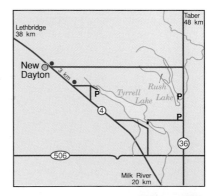

Fish and Wildlife Division,
Lethbridge 381-5281
St. Mary's River Irrigation District,
Lethbridge 328-4401

Outpost Wetlands Natural Area

Common wood nymph

Common snipe

Below the slopes of Chief Mountain, Boundary Creek flows past aspen forests, rolling grassland, bedrock outcrops and patches of horizontal juniper, opening into a large wetland bisected by the Canada-U.S. boundary. This is a good spot for viewing waterbirds such as the common snipe, known for its unusual courtship display. In spring, an eerie, tremulous whistling can often be heard over the wetlands. The male flies high into the air, and then begins a rapid zig-zagging descent with wings folded back. Rushing air makes its two outer tail-feathers vibrate, creating the sound.

The 65-hectare site, adjacent to Police Outpost Provincial Park, contains a system of unimproved trails, good for nature observation, birdwatching, hiking and cross-country skiing. Outpost is an example of foothills parkland, and has an interesting mix of flora and fauna.

Unusual varieties of species here include northern pocket gopher, Richardson's and columbian ground squirrels, sandhill crane, blue grouse, cinnamon teal, northern waterthrush, American goldfinch and vesper sparrow.

Directions: Access through Police Outpost Provincial Park following Hwy. 2 south of Cardston for 6 km, then turn west and follow park signs.

Public Lands Division,
Lethbridge 329-5486
Provincial Parks Service,
Police Outpost Provincial Park 653-2522

Waterton Lakes National Park

This site, where prairie meets mountains abruptly, has the greatest density and variety of wildlife of any Rocky Mountain destination. Twenty-two of Alberta's 26 orchid species occur here: the greatest concentration of species in the province. Golden eagles soar above the mountains, and bald eagles are common during migration.

At the Waterton townsite, look for American dippers, violet-green swallows, MacGillivray's warblers, and rufous and calliope hummingbirds, as well as mule deer and bighorn sheep. Wolverine and cougar are occasionally observed.

At Cameron Lake, listen for the songs of Swainson's, hermit and varied thrushes in the evening. Scan the snowslide areas of the mountain slopes across Cameron Lake with binoculars for the best chance of seeing grizzly bears

Indian paintbrush

anywhere in Alberta. Bears are always unpredictable, so observe the caution signs and keep your distance.

Pause at the active osprey nest near the park entrance gate, and look for the cliff swallow colony at the bridge.

Grizzly bear

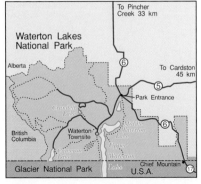

Canadian Parks Service,
Park Office 859-2224

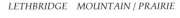

East Porcupine Hills

Subalpine fir cones

This unique area, named for the spears of Douglas fir and limber pine which rise along the crests of the hills, combines four distinct vegetation patterns for a diversified wildlife habitat. Characteristics of montane forest, subalpine forest, aspen parkland and prairie grassland are all found in this area.

A wide variety of wildflowers and shrubs, from grouseberry and thimbleberry, through meadow rue and sticky geranium, to dryland species such as ground juniper and shrubby cinquefoil, are found at various elevations. Look for mountain chickadees, crossbills, and snowshoe hares at the higher elevations. Coniferous forests are home to red-breasted nuthatches and spruce grouse. In the oatgrass and fescue prairie, watch for red-tailed hawks and ground squirrels, wapiti and mule deer.

Look for pine siskins and yellow-pine chipmunks in the limber pine forests of dry south-facing slopes.

Mountain chickadee

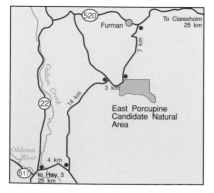

Alberta Forest Service,
Blairmore 381-5473
Fish and Wildlife Division,
Claresholm 625-3301

Big Sagebrush

Xanthoria (orange) and Lecanora (grey)

Clark's nutcracker

This area provides ideal conditions for many species otherwise uncommon in Alberta. Patchworks of pine and poplar forests, and grassy and shrubby glades on the river valley bottoms rise into rubble and bedrock outcrops supporting scrub aspen, lodgepole pine, subalpine meadows and open rockland. Vegetation thins toward the crest into lichen-covered boulders and alpine cushion plants.

The varied habitats support many different plants and animals. Plant lovers should have little trouble finding some of the 35 species that are rare in Alberta, ten of which are rare in Canada, including the delicate, creamy white Mariposa lily. Blue grouse, Clark's nutcracker, Townsend's solitaire and varied thrush are some of the area's many bird species, and with luck you may see soaring golden eagles, colourful lazuli buntings or calliope hummingbirds.

Columbian ground squirrels, golden-mantled ground squirrels, and mule deer are easily spotted, and look for pika, moose, wapiti and bighorn sheep. Grizzly and black bears are also found here.

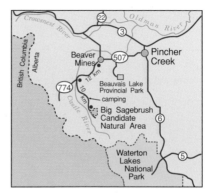

Road access from Secondary Hwy. 774 is rough and may be restricted by snow during winter.

Alberta Forest Service, Blairmore 562-7331
Public Lands Division, Edmonton 427-5209

Crowsnest Lake and River

Alpine larch

C. WERSHLER

Long-toed salamander

J. BUTLER

Crowsnest Lake, one of the deepest in Alberta, lies near the top of historic Crowsnest Pass. The pass area is low enough to support a montane forest of Douglas fir and lodgepole pine, mixed with aspen groves and grassland. The area has many species of wildflowers found only in this corner of Alberta, such as umbrella-plants, beard-tongues, and yellow and red monkey-flowers.

As the lowest crossing of the Rockies in the region, the pass provides habitat for birds normally found further west, such as the house finch and the red-naped sapsucker, which is closely related to the more widespread yellow-bellied sapsucker. Numerous ducks, geese and swans can often be seen on the lake, as can loons and grebes. Look for long-toed salamanders, spotted frogs and boreal toads along wetland areas. Bighorn sheep frequently graze nearby.

The Crowsnest River has rainbow, cutthroat and brown trout, as well as bull trout and mountain whitefish.

Fish and Wildlife Division, Alberta Forest Service, Blairmore 562-7331
Public Lands Division, Lethbridge 329-5486

Beehive Natural Area

The more than 800 hectares of pristine old-growth forests within this vast natural area provide a specialized habitat for such species as marten, fisher, woodpeckers and wood warblers.

Mount Beehive

The entire protected area, situated along the Continental Divide and eastern slopes of the Rockies, is a diverse complex of cool, dark lodgepole pine and subalpine fir forests, fast-flowing trout streams, windy alpine meadows, scree slopes, bare ridges, moist herb meadows and undisturbed old spruce-fir forests. Prominent inhabitants are grizzly and black bears, wapiti, moose, and bighorn sheep.

Birds include Townsend's solitaires, Townsend's warblers, Hammond's flycatchers, Clark's nutcrackers, rosy finches and white-tailed ptarmigans.

Wildlife viewing in this huge area may require energetic hiking or cross-country skiing on the many kilometres of trail. Routes start at the Oldman River and ascend Beehive Creek and Cache Creek with good spots for fishing. Another route parallels the Continental Divide.

Western spring beauty

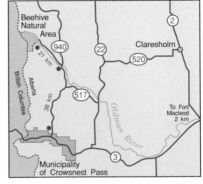

Access to the road from Hwy. 940 to the beginning of the natural area may be restricted by snow during winter.

Alberta Forest Service, Blairmore 562-7331
Public Lands Division, Edmonton 427-5209

MEDICINE HAT
Grassland / Water

Hoodoos and sandstone outcrops form a backdrop for soaring golden eagles and prairie falcons. Pronghorn range across the prairie, and distinctive wildflowers grow in rock crevices and along roadside ditches.

This most arid segment of the province, the short-grass prairie region, supports majestic cottonwood trees along its broad, deep river valleys. In the southeast corner of the province, the forest and open woodland cover of the Cypress Hills are reminiscent of the foothills. Here, deer, elk and moose seek refuge.

Wildlife Viewing Site (showing page number)	66
Major Roads	39
Cities and Towns	●
Provincial Park	⬚
Ecozones	
Short Grass	
Mixed Grass	
Aspen Parkland	
Boreal Foothills	

50 kilometres

Police Point Park

A network of interpretive trails provides access to this floodplain woodland with its extensive shrub and grasslands, which is home to a wide variety of nesting and migrating birds. The gnarled plains cottonwood trees are a distinctive feature of the area.

American kestrels nest in the cavities of old trees at Police Point, and prairie falcons and golden eagles are also present year-round. Songbirds such as warblers, wrens and swallows particularly favour the combination of shrub and woodland habitat. Along the South Saskatchewan River, look for wood ducks in spring migration, and wintering mallards, common goldeneyes and, occasionally, bald eagles.

Watch for Nuttall's cottontails, porcupines, red foxes and white-tailed deer, all of which are resident at Police Point throughout the year. Consult the Interpretive Centre for up-to-date information on wildlife activities and rare bird sightings in this area.

Plains cottonwood

C. WERSHLER

Directions: Access from Trans-Canada Hwy. via Gershaw Drive to 3 St. SE.
Police Point Interpretive Centre,
Medicine Hat 529-6225

Cypress Hills Provincial Park

Cypress Hills

This unglaciated plateau is an island of boreal foothills forest, surrounded by dry mixed grassland. The combination of plant and animal species is unlike any other in Canada.

Fourteen orchid species can be found in the park, including Franklin's lady's-slipper.

More than two hundred species of birds have been recorded, of which half nest in this area. Gray catbirds, dusky flycatchers and hairy woodpeckers inhabit the forested areas. Wood warbler species include the ovenbird, American redstart and MacGillivray's and orange-crowned warblers. Wild turkeys have been introduced. The pink-sided race of the dark-eyed junco nests nowhere else in Canada, and only in this part of Alberta can you hear the common poorwill call at night.

Double-crested cormorants and white-winged scoters can be found at Elkwater Lake, along with migratory waterfowl. The Spruce Coulee Reservoir is among the best sites for bird viewing.

Wapiti, moose, mule deer, white-tailed deer and pronghorn can be seen in the area.

Pronghorn

Provincial Parks Service,
Park Office 893-3777
Fish and Wildlife Division
Medicine Hat 529-3680

MEDICINE HAT   GRASSLAND / WATER

Red Rock Coulee Natural Area

A community of wildlife has adapted to harsh conditions in this dry, barren terrain of badlands, hoodoos and large red boulders. Rock wrens find crevices in rocks; prairie rattlesnakes seek out holes. Clumps of sagebrush and juniper cling to the eroding walls. Evening primroses with large, pink petals grow in clay, and buffalo beans with their vivid yellow flowers survive amid the weathered shale.

Sand lily

The most remarkable features of the area are the reddish, rounded sandstone rocks that may measure up to 2.5 metres across. These sandstone concretions are believed to be among the largest of their kind in the world.

The area's birds include lark buntings, horned larks and grasshopper sparrows. The flute-like songs of western meadowlarks can often be heard from spring through summer. These birds hide their nests in the long grass by weaving canopies of concealing vegetation overhead. Look for white-tailed jackrabbits, mule deer and pronghorn, as well as short-horned lizards and scorpions, which are rare in Alberta.

Short-horned lizard

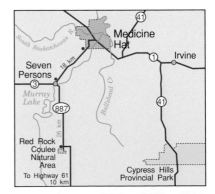

Public Lands Division,
Medicine Hat 529-3677
Public Lands Division,
Edmonton 427-5209

Pakowki Lake

Swallowtail butterfly

The west arm of this intermittent lake, one of the largest lakes in southern Alberta, provides some of the finest marsh habitat in the province.

Double-crested cormorants and black-crowned night-herons can be easily seen from the northern shore, along with marsh wrens, cinnamon teals and American bitterns. Sightings of such rare species as the Eurasian wigeon, black-necked stilt and snowy egret have been recorded. White-faced ibis, exceedingly rare elsewhere in Canada, have nested at the lake.

Pronghorn can be seen in the surrounding uplands along the northern shore. Badgers and coyotes are common in the area, as are striped skunks and porcupines. Plains garter snakes may be found in the immediate area of the lake.

White-tailed jack rabbit

M. BAILEY

PROVINCIAL PARKS SERVICE

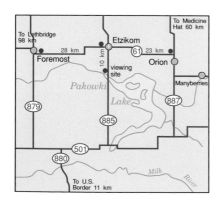

Fish and Wildlife Division,
Medicine Hat 529-3680
Fish and Wildlife Division,
Foremost 867-3826

Writing-on-Stone Provincial Park

Prairie falcon

Plains spadefoot toad tadpole

Spectacular sandstone outcrops, mature cottonwood trees, diverse coulee systems, and the scenic Milk River make this park one of Alberta's richest wildlife viewing locations. The park contains 265 recorded species of plants. The 60 recorded nesting bird species include the rock wren, rufous-sided towhee, golden eagle, prairie falcon, and others whose ranges barely reach the province, such as the lazuli bunting. Sit on sandstone hoodoos west of the campground in the evening and listen for coyotes and great horned owls and watch for common nighthawk activity. Nighthawks can be seen resting by day along horizontal limbs of the cottonwoods.

Many of the park's 22 mammal species are common and easily seen, including Nuttall's cottontails, white-tailed jackrabbits, mule deer, porcupines and yellow-bellied marmots. Western rattlesnakes and bull snakes are common in some locations. Many rare wildlife species occur, including the Delaware skipper and two-tailed swallowtail butterflies, the western small-footed bat, and the bobcat.

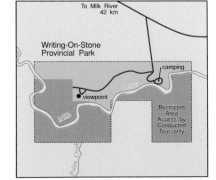

Provincial Park Service,
Park Office 647-2364/647-2252
Fish and Wildlife Division,
Foremost 867-3826

MEDICINE HAT GRASSLAND / WATER

Lake Newell

As the only major reservoir in the area, Lake Newell attracts many species of prairie waterfowl and water birds. It has one of the largest nesting populations of Canada geese in Alberta and is also a nesting site for dabbling and diving ducks. Several protected islands are used by colonies of nesting birds including double-crested cormorants, American white pelicans and California and ring-billed gulls. Visitors are not permitted on these islands.

Double-crested cormorant colony

The best viewing areas are along the east shore, where Kinbrook Island Provincial Park is connected to the mainland by a causeway. The marsh areas provide habitat for ducks, coots, rails, bitterns, grebes and geese.

The native grasslands surrounding the lake are good places to spot pronghorn, burrowing owls, long-billed curlews and chestnut-collared longspurs. Check carefully for black widow spiders in abandoned ground squirrel and badger burrows.

Swen Bayer Peninsula is located south of the provincial park. A self-guided, interpretive trail leads around the scenic peninsula with its sheltered bays, marshes, grassland and long stretches of shoreline.

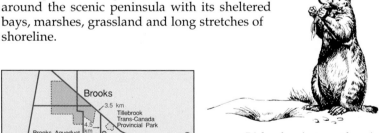

Richardson's ground squirrel

Dinosaur Provincial Park (facing page)
EGON BORK

Provincial Parks Service,
Kinbrook Island Provincial Park 362-2962
Fish and Wildlife Division,
Lethbridge 381-5281

(Map:)
Brooks
3.5 km
Tillebrook
Trans-Canada
Provincial Park
4.5 km
Brooks Aqueduct
Marshes
(36)
(873)
Macbeth
(542)
(1)
To
Medicine
Hat
77 km
Kinbrook
Island
Provincial
Park
Tilley
(876)
Lake Newell
Swen Bayer
Peninsula
(535)
To Taber
67 km

MEDICINE HAT   GRASSLAND / WATER

Dinosaur Provincial Park

This World Heritage Site contains internationally famous dinosaur bone concentrations, Canada's largest protected badland areas, and a wide variety of wildlife, including over 140 bird species.

Great horned owl

PROVINCIAL PARKS SERVICE

Explore the Cottonwood Flats Trail and campground to see mule deer, Canada geese, eastern and western kingbirds, rufous-sided towhees and northern orioles. Watch for belted kingfishers, great blue herons, great horned owls, brown thrashers and yellow-breasted chats near the Red Deer River.

Take a guided bus tour into the Nature Preserve or hike the Badlands Trail to see rock wrens, Say's phoebes, mountain bluebirds, prairie falcons and possibly a golden eagle or ferruginous hawk. On the prairie, look for Swainson's hawks, long-billed curlews, marbled godwits and horned larks.

In winter, watch for snow buntings, common redpolls and pronghorn. Waterfowl are abundant during spring and fall migrations. Following spring rains, listen for the rarely seen plains spadefoot toad. Bull snakes and prairie rattlesnakes are present here in summer. In May and June, blooming cactus and wildflowers are spectacular.

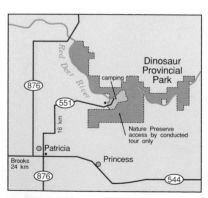

Rock wren

Provincial Parks Service,
Park Office 378-4587
Fish and Wildlife Division,
Brooks 362-5551

MEDICINE HAT   GRASSLAND / WATER

NORTHEAST
Lakeland / Boreal

Sites in this region range from parkland and farmland in the south, through extensive boreal mixed-wood forest and muskeg, to deltaic wetlands and lichen woodlands in the far northeast.

Here, white and black spruce, jack pine, trembling aspen, balsam poplar and white birch dominate the dense tree cover. The many lakes, rivers and streams support great blue herons, ospreys and pelicans, as well as bear and moose and dozens of spawning fish species.

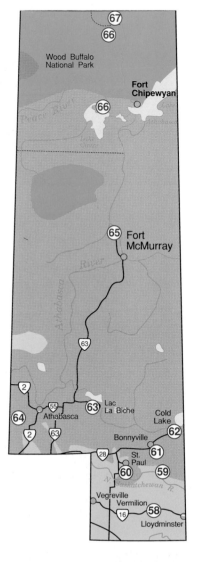

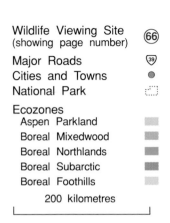

Wildlife Viewing Site (showing page number)	66
Major Roads	39
Cities and Towns	●
National Park	⋮⋮⋮

Ecozones
Aspen Parkland
Boreal Mixedwood
Boreal Northlands
Boreal Subarctic
Boreal Foothills

200 kilometres

Vermilion Provincial Park

Red-tailed hawk

The Vermilion River meanders through a wide, steep valley with aspen forests blanketing the north-facing slopes, and prairie grasslands covering the drier south-facing slopes. Further on, a dam has widened the river, flooding about half the valley floor within the park. Visitors can stay overnight at the campground and hike a trail in the early morning for some exceptional wildlife viewing.

Along the Aspen, Wild Rose and Cathedral trails, look for white-tailed deer, red foxes, Franklin's ground squirrels, porcupines and ruffed grouse. Richardson's ground squirrels are common on the Fescue Trail, and you may also see northern harriers, red-tailed hawks and short-eared owls.

The Lakeside Trail along the reservoir offers opportunities to view Canada geese, great blue herons, American bitterns, shorebirds and various ducks, as well as mink, muskrats and beavers.

The grassland environment on the north side of the river is a good place to look for coyotes, Sprague's pipits and savannah and vesper sparrows.

Provincial Parks Service, Park Office 853-8159
Fish and Wildlife Division, Vermilion 853-8137

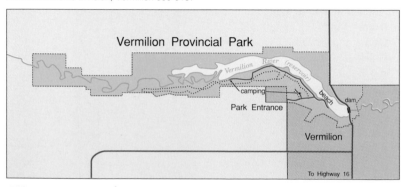

NORTHEAST LAKELAND / BOREAL

Whitney Lakes Provincial Park

Yellow-headed blackbird chick   *Long-horned beetle*

This park contains an intriguing mosaic of landforms, including eskers, sand hills, hummocky terrain, and lake basins, on which several types of vegetation have developed: jack pine stands, meadows, aspen groves, willow thickets, marshes, fens and mixed-wood forests.

Of 148 bird species recorded here, 62 frequent lakes and wetlands; these include great blue herons, pied-billed grebes and yellow-headed blackbirds. Whooping cranes and numerous ducks and geese have been observed during migration. Borden Lake and the bays on the west side of Laurier Lake are excellent points from which to view such birds.

Seventeen species of warblers and vireos inhabit the mixed-wood forests and aspen groves, including the Connecticut warbler. Look for Tennessee warblers, northern flickers and least chipmunks in the jack pine forests, and common snipes, palm warblers and swamp sparrows in the fens. The marshes are home to wood frogs, muskrats and mink.

The four major lakes in the park contain yellow perch, northern pike and walleye.

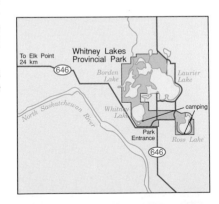

Provincial Parks Service,
Park Office 943-3761
Fish and Wildlife Division,
St. Paul 645-6313

NORTHEAST   LAKELAND / BOREAL

59

Therien Lakes

The numerous islands and bays in the upper and lower lakes provide habitat for many wildlife species.

The lakes are used for staging by Arctic nesters such as the ruddy turnstone and other shorebirds. Rare sightings have included Barrow's goldeneyes and hooded mergansers, among others. Visit the viewing stand at Upper Therien Lake on the outskirts of St. Paul, and the campground on the lower lake.

The nesting islands of ring-billed and California gulls, and the nesting colony of double-crested cormorants are particularly sensitive to disturbance during the breeding season. Visitors should stay clear of these areas.

Great blue herons, black-crowned night-herons, Canada geese and American white pelicans are other spectacular birds found here.

Beavers, muskrats and mink inhabit the wetlands and shallow bays of this region.

J. BUTLER

Mink

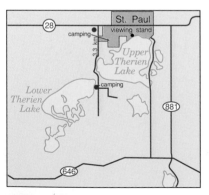

Fish and Wildlife Division,
St. Paul 645-6313

Jessie Lake

Great densities of shorebirds and waterfowl are found at Jessie Lake during spring and fall migrations. The lake is an important staging area for migrating birds. The marsh and aspen parkland along its margins provide abundant nesting sites for both shore and song birds. Among

the latter are yellow-headed blackbirds and both savannah and Le Conte's sparrows. American avocets, willets, marbled godwits and greater and lesser yellowlegs are found along the margins from spring to fall. Eared and horned grebes nest on the lake together with a large colony of Franklin's gulls and many species of ducks.

The two islands in the southwest section of the lake provide unusual concentrations of nesting ducks, and are therefore particularly sensitive.

Moose Lake to the west and Muriel Lake to the south also provide excellent viewing opportunities.

American avocet and chick

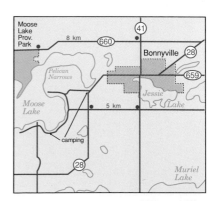

Fish and Wildlife Division,
Bonnyville 826-3142
Town of Bonnyville,
826-3496

NORTHEAST   LAKELAND / BOREAL

Cold Lake Provincial Park

One of the largest nesting colonies of western grebes in Alberta inhabits shallow Centre Bay adjacent to Cold Lake Provincial Park. The entire park is rich with a variety of wildlife habitats, due to its location on a partly wooded peninsula that juts out into the southern end of Cold Lake.

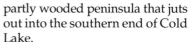

Cold Lake

Cold Lake is known for its lake trout and walleye, and about two hundred bird species have been sighted in the area. The shallow, protected bays with their warmer water are a good place to see waterfowl such as teals and mallards. A hiking trail leads to an observation platform overlooking Hall's Lagoon.

The park is inhabited by many perching birds, especially wood warblers, sparrows, flycatchers, thrushes and vireos. In forested areas, watch for brown creepers, solitary vireos, golden-crowned kinglets, western tanagers, and Cape May, blackburnian and bay-breasted warblers. In the fens south of Centre Bay, listen for sora, and look for sign of mink along the shore.

Snowshoe hare

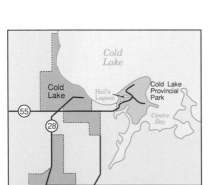

Provincial Parks Service,
Park Office 639-3341
Fish and Wildlife Division,
Cold Lake 639-3377

62

Sir Winston Churchill Provincial Park

Old-growth forests of white and black spruce, balsam fir, birch and poplar make this perhaps the finest location for viewing boreal forest birds in Alberta. The island-to-mainland causeway is an excellent birding spot.

Twenty species of breeding wood warblers occur here, including black-throated green, palm, magnolia, mourning, bay-breasted, Cape May, and blackburnian warblers. The conifers are home to white-winged crossbills, Swainson's and hermit thrushes, and olive-sided flycatchers. Northern saw-whet, barred, and even boreal owls may be heard at night.

From Pelican Viewpoint on the north side of the island one can observe the American white pelicans, double-crested cormorants and California gulls that frequent Pelican Island some distance to the north of the park.

There are Franklin's ground squirrels in the picnic area. In spring, toads trill east of the Long Point trail, which is the best birding trail. The last week of May into early June is the best time to listen for bird song.

Sir Winston Churchill Provincial Park

Blackburnian warbler

Directions: Access from town of Lac La Biche to the northeast on secondary highway 868 for 3 to 4 km and then follow signs.

Provincial Parks Service,
Park Office 623-4144
Fish and Wildlife Division,
Lac La Biche 623-5247

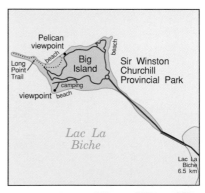

Cross Lake Provincial Park

A hike along one of the park's trails will take you through mixed-wood stands of poplar, spruce and pine. Here you will often see snowshoe hares, red squirrels, white-throated sparrows, ruffed grouse and several warbler species, as well as moose, deer and bears. During winter, bohemian waxwings, evening and pine grosbeaks and white-winged crossbills feed on the various fruit-bearing trees and shrubs.

One of the most significant features of the park is its resident birds of prey. Ospreys and bald eagles can best be glimpsed as they forage for supper along the shoreline or out on the lake.

Great blue herons and ospreys nest around Steele Lake. Don't approach too closely, as your presence may lead to nest abandonment and loss of young.

The French Creek fish ladder near the west end of Steele Lake is an excellent site to view the fish-spawning runs of northern pike, as well as longnose and white suckers in May and June.

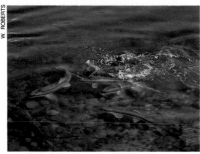

Spawning longnose suckers

Forest tent caterpillar

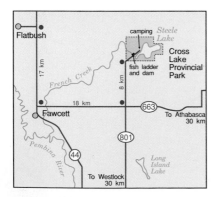

Provincial Parks Service,
Park Office (seasonal) 681-2331
Provincial Parks Service,
Lesser Slave Lake Prov. Park 849-7100

NORTHEAST LAKELAND / BOREAL

Poplar Creek

The Poplar Creek gravel pit covers approximately 300 hectares. When areas of it have been fully mined for their aggregate deposits, they are allowed to return to a semi-natural state. This process, known as succession, creates habitat for many wildlife species.

Wild rose

The site consists of shrubland and open grassland areas, surrounded by aspen and white and black spruce stands. Look for wild rose bushes, blueberries and raspberries, as well as highbush cranberries and saskatoons.

Canada geese, great blue herons, sandhill cranes and other interesting bird species visit the area each year. Throughout the forested areas and road access sites, view white-tailed deer, black bears and, possibly, coyotes. Watch for chipmunks and squirrels darting across the roads and through the trees.

In the winter, deer may be seen browsing shrubs in snow-covered grassy areas. At dusk, you may catch a glimpse of a great horned owl as it swoops down on a snowshoe hare.

White spruce

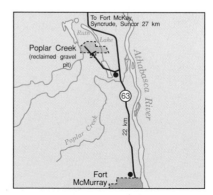

Alberta Forest Service,
Fort McMurray 743-7125
Fish and Wildlife Division,
Fort McMurray 743-7200

Wood Buffalo National Park

The great wetlands that receive the waters of the Peace and Athabasca river systems along the eastern edge of this park represent the largest inland freshwater delta in the world. Four major North American flyways converge on this vast nesting area, a destination for countless flocks of migrant birds.

The Salt Plains Overview overlooks a bizarre landscape of saline meadows and grassland. Peregrine falcons, bald and golden eagles and many species of songbirds, waterfowl and shorebirds can be seen here. This is the only nesting ground in the world for the rare whooping crane.

Established in 1922 as a protected area for Canada's remaining wood bison, Wood Buffalo is the largest national park in Canada. Moose, woodland caribou and wolves are common here.

Access is limited to water routes in summer and ice roads in winter, but the difficult journey is rewarded by unequalled photographic and viewing opportunities.

Golden eagle

Directions: (May 1 to Oct. 31) access Salt Plains Overview by following Hwy. 5 from Fort Smith for 30 km, then turn south and follow signs for 10 km.

Canadian Parks Service, Fort Smith 872-2349
Canadian Parks Service,
Fort Chipewyan 697-3662

NORTHEAST LAKELAND / BOREAL

Slave River - Mountain Rapids

Here the ecosystems of the Precambrian Shield and the Western Sedimentary Basin meet, fostering an unusually diverse assembly of flora and fauna.

This is the most northerly nesting place in North America for American white pelicans: their nesting islands in the Slave River can be seen from a viewpoint on the west bank. Within ten kilometres are four sets of spectacular rapids where the powerful river meets an outcrop of Precambrian granite. Portions of the portage route of early explorers and fur traders are still visible. This is a spawning area for northern lamprey, northern pike, whitefish and goldeye, among other fish.

As much of the soil is sandy, jack pine and various grasses have

American white pelicans

Northern pike

established themselves here. White spruce, white birch and balsam poplar grow along the river. The undergrowth contains highbush cranberry, alder, wild rose, bunchberry, raspberry, honeysuckle and willow. Calypso orchids can also be found.

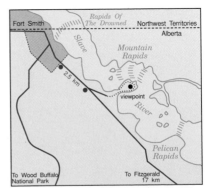

Canadian Parks Service,
Fort Smith 872-2349
Alberta Forest Service,
Fort Chipewyan 697-3762

NORTHWEST
Parkland / Boreal

As many as two hundred bird species have been recorded in parts of northwestern Alberta, and several lakeside sites offer viewing platforms and interpretive programs for visitors.

As one travels north through this region, aspen parkland gives way to aspen and spruce boreal forest, which covers most of the northern half of the province. The successional forests and organic wetlands of the Peace River district provide habitats for sandhill cranes, northern goshawks, bear, moose and deer. Sphagnum mosses, Labrador tea and cranberry proliferate in the bogs and fens throughout the northwest peatlands.

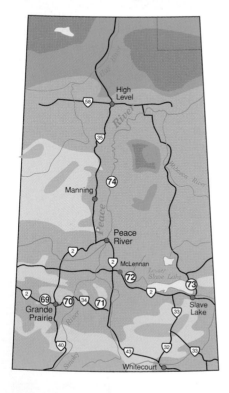

Wildlife Viewing Site ⑥⑥
(showing page number)
Major Roads -⟨39⟩-
Cities and Towns ●
National Park ⌒
Ecozones
  Aspen Parkland
  Boreal Mixedwood
  Boreal Foothills
  Boreal Uplands
  Boreal Northlands
  Boreal Subarctic
    200 kilometres

Saskatoon Island Provincial Park

Coyote

This scenic area, once an island in Saskatoon Lake, now consists of a land bridge separating Saskatoon and Little lakes.

The park includes several habitats — aspen forest, wetlands, grassland patches and the best remaining example of saskatoon shrubland in northern Alberta. The dense shrubbery is loaded with delicious berries in July.

Birdwatchers will enjoy viewing the large numbers of grassland, forest and lakeside birds. A bird-viewing platform by Little Lake, complete with telescope, overlooks the nesting areas of several species of waterfowl including the rare trumpeter swan. Decreasing lake levels threaten the swans' habitat, but immature trumpeter swans may still be seen on either lake. In autumn, hundreds of trumpeter and tundra swans converge on Saskatoon Lake for three weeks before their migration south.

The park is a year-round home to snowshoe hares, weasels, woodchucks, muskrats, beavers and deer, and is visited frequently by coyotes.

Muskoseepi Park is located in the heart of nearby Grande Prairie. A trail winds along the Bear Creek Ravine, offering an attractive nature walk. The park pavilion is the centre for interpretive displays and family events year-round.

Trumpeter swan

Provincial Parks Service,
Park Office (seasonal) 766-2636
Provincial Parks Service,
Young's Point Provincial Park 957-2699

Kleskun Hill Natural Area

Northern saw-whet owl

Prickly pear cactus

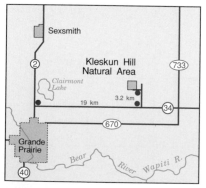

Kleskun Hill rises a hundred metres above the plains surrounding Grande Prairie. It is one of the most extensive areas of native upland grassland remaining in the Peace River parkland. It is also the most northern occurrence of a badlands landscape in Alberta.

Northern saw-whet owls, American kestrels, black terns, Swainson's and gray-cheeked thrushes and sharp-tailed grouse are characteristic birds of the region.

The 65-hectare natural area offers scenic vistas and opportunities for pleasant nature walks to examine the many species of prairie and badlands plants that are near their northern distribution limits, including prickly pear cactus. There is a picnic site at the south end.

Several "skeletonized" hills dot the area. Each is banded with alternating layers of clays, sands and narrow seams of coal which represent sediments deposited under prehistoric lakes and seas. Look for fossilized fragments of dinosaur bones and wood.

Public Lands Division,
Grande Prairie 538-5260
Fish and Wildlife Division,
Grande Prairie 538-5265

Young's Point Provincial Park

Over 150 bird species nest in or visit this boreal park which encompasses seven kilometres of shoreline on Sturgeon Lake. Mixedwood forests combine with cattail and arum shoreline in the 1090-hectare park.

A platform east of the campground permits excellent viewing of beaver lodges and muskrat push-ups. Mature coniferous forests provide a home for many wood warblers. Songbirds, waterfowl and shorebirds are readily visible from both the platform and the shore trails. By midsummer the ponds in the park are likely to show a continuous green carpet of floating duckweed.

Damselfly

Beaver cuttings

Moose and white-tailed and mule deer are frequently sighted along the extensive park trail system. The Eagle Creek trail is recommended for sightings of bald eagles and both great horned and great gray owls. In June and September, look for migrating warblers, shorebirds and waterfowl.

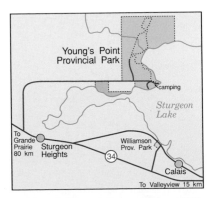

Provincial Parks Service,
Park Office 957-2699
Fish and Wildlife Division,
Valleyview 524-3605

Winagami / Kimiwan Lakes

Evening birdwatching

Located near the town of McLennan, the self-proclaimed Bird Capital of Canada, these lakes provide exceptional viewing opportunities, particularly during spring and fall migrations. Bald eagles converge here in the fall, preying on fish and ducks. Look for the eagles in early morning during freeze-up, when as many as twelve have been seen at one time.

More than 200 species of birds, both nesting and migratory, have been recorded at Winagami Lake Provincial Park. Stroll along the boreal forest trail that leads from the boat launch to a raised bird viewing platform, from which you can observe nesting colonies of grebes, sandpipers, gulls and many species of ducks.

Twenty-three kilometres northwest of the park lies teardrop-shaped Kimiwan Lake. It is well worth a visit to see the spectacular concentrations of waterfowl and migratory shorebirds, which include rare visitors such as the cinnamon teal. Predatory birds in the area include merlin and northern goshawk — a superb hunter.

Pintail duckling

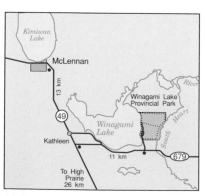

Provincial Parks Service,
Winagami Provincial Park 523-2427
Public Lands Division,
High Prairie 523-6580 (Re: Kimiwan Lake)

Lesser Slave Lake Provincial Park

Lesser Slave Lake

Mixed-wood boreal forest, fens, marshes and sand dunes provide habitat for many wildlife species, including more than 150 species of birds.

The forests contain black bears, mule and white-tailed deer, martens, ruffed grouse, great horned owls, white-winged crossbills and numerous wood warblers during summer; Canada lynx and gray wolves are most conspicuous in winter.

Red squirrels, snowshoe hares and least chipmunks are common throughout the park. Marshy areas are home to mink, muskrats, beavers and, occasionally, moose. Waterfowl, shorebirds and other water birds may be seen along the shoreline.

Grizzly bears and Canada lynx have been observed in the Marten Mountain area. Balsam fir stands harbour many plant species characteristic of high rainfall forests, including the bizarre devil's-club, with sharp spines covering its stem and the undersides of its maple leaf-shaped leaves. Bald eagles and American white pelicans may be seen at the lakeshore and beach areas of Dog Island.

Twin-flowers

Provincial Parks Service,
Park Office 849-7100
Fish and Wildlife Division,
Slave Lake 849-7110

73

Notikewin Provincial Park

The mighty Peace River runs by this attractive provincial park bordered by the mature forest of the valley below and the plateau above. One can observe sandhill cranes and also several species of raptors which make their homes here.

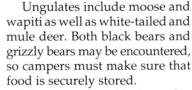

Ungulates include moose and wapiti as well as white-tailed and mule deer. Both black bears and grizzly bears may be encountered, so campers must make sure that food is securely stored.

The campground is situated in a forest of balsam poplar and white spruce, often with ostrich fern communities in the understory. Cavity-nesting bird species, including a variety of woodpeckers, may also be seen throughout the forest.

Lichen (peltigera species)

Visitors can cross the Notikewin River (good fishing at the mouth for walleye, pike and goldeye) and hike through the southern end of the park where lodgepole and jack pine predominate. The open understory provides a variety of plant species in a spectacular setting along the banks of the Peace.

Moose

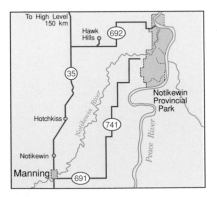

Provincial Parks Service,
Park Office (seasonal) 836-2792
Provincial Parks Service,
Moonshine Lake Provincial Park 864-2266

NORTHWEST PARKLAND / BOREAL

JASPER / BANFF
Mountains / Foothills

From foothills to mountain peaks, the combination of wildlife species in this region varies according to the elevation and the climate. Canyons, waterfalls and hot springs add to the richness of wildlife viewing opportunities here.

On the lower slopes, forests of white spruce and lodgepole pine predominate, while higher up the forest vegetation gives way to wildflower-laden alpine meadows, stunted krummholz trees, and barren rock. Pika, ptarmigan and mountain sheep are among the inhabitants of this craggy country, which is one of the most dramatic viewing locations in the world.

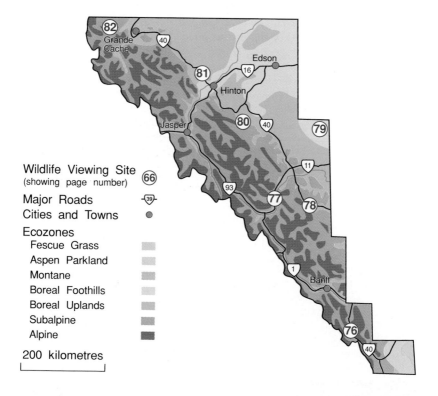

Wildlife Viewing Site
(showing page number)   (66)

Major Roads   -(39)-

Cities and Towns   ●

Ecozones
  Fescue Grass
  Aspen Parkland
  Montane
  Boreal Foothills
  Boreal Uplands
  Subalpine
  Alpine

200 kilometres

Peter Lougheed Provincial Park

Yellow heather (above)
White-tailed ptarmigan (left)

One of the best places to see bighorn sheep is at King Creek, where a mineral lick also attracts the occasional deer, wapiti or moose. Ungulates, aquatic mammals and various birds may be observed at the Pocaterra Fen, a large, wet, grassy meadow and pond area. From the Sawmill day-use and overflow camping site, you can scan Kent Ridge and the nearby slopes for mountain goats, bighorn sheep and wapiti. Bring binoculars or a spotting scope. In spring you might even see a grizzly bear.

Watch pikas at close range along the Rock Glacier interpretive trail near Highwood Pass. Here you'll also find glacier lilies blooming on the avalanche tracks in May, while valerians, Indian paintbrushes and heathers are in full glory in July and early August.

The many different species of birds found here include bald and golden eagles, mountain bluebird, varied thrush, white-tailed ptarmigan, blue grouse, osprey, harlequin duck, Steller's jay, Clark's nutcracker, and American dipper.

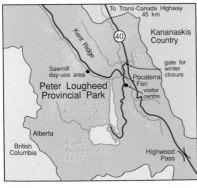

Pika

Kananaskis Country,
Park Office 591-7222
Fish and Wildlife Division,
Calgary 297-6423

JASPER / BANFF MOUNTAINS / FOOTHILLS

White Goat and Siffleur Wilderness Areas

Some of the most rugged and spectacular alpine terrain in Alberta lies within the vast White Goat (44,457 hectares) and Siffleur (41,214 hectares) Wilderness Areas in the Front Ranges of the Rockies.

Large mammals in the valleys and on the lower slopes include moose, wapiti, white-tailed and mule deer, black bears, and coyotes. Other residents that can be more difficult to spot include grizzly bears, cougars, wolves and wolverines. In alpine and upper sub-alpine areas, look for mountain goats, woodland caribou, golden-mantled ground squirrels, bighorn sheep, hoary marmots and pikas, as well as white-tailed ptarmigans, gray-crowned rosy

Siffleur Falls

finches, water pipits and horned larks. Eagles range throughout these areas.

Hikers should be experienced and well prepared for wilderness travel before setting out on any of the several access trails. The routes are challenging and remote, and many of the animals encountered here have little fear of humans.

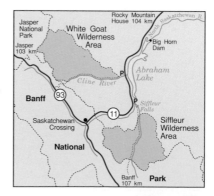

Caribou

Provincial Parks Service,
Rimbey 843-2545
Fish and Wildlife Division,
Rocky Mountain House 845-8230

Ram Falls Recreation Area

Bighorn sheep can be seen on the slopes of the 2850-metre Ram Range throughout the year — often near Ram Falls, where the river plunges 20 metres over a thin layer of hard sandstone.

A principal viewing location is within a short walk of the Ram Falls campsite, on the north side of the river, downstream from the falls. The canyon itself offers a dramatic view of eroded shale and sandstone, and golden eagles may be seen soaring on the canyon air currents. In the fall, bald eagles, merlins and American kestrels wing south along the eastern slopes of the Rocky Mountains.

Red squirrels are abundant in the pine and spruce forests, and

Ram Falls

Red squirrel

black bears may be seen from mid-spring to late fall.

Look for both cutthroat trout, which rise to the surface to feed on mayflies and caddis flies, and American dippers, dark wren-like birds that feed on insects in the rushing water.

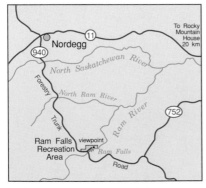

Fish and Wildlife Division,
Rocky Mountain House 845-8230
Alberta Forestry Service,
Rocky Mountain House 845-8250

Brazeau Reservoir

Coniferous trees in this area provide excellent habitat for cavity-nesting birds such as tree swallows and common goldeneyes. The trees are also inhabited by nesting great blue herons and ospreys.

Ravens nest on the cliffs south of the main dam, and there are particularly rewarding birdwatching opportunities along the south edge of the canal. Northern pike can occasionally be seen in shallow water.

The reservoir houses the greatest concentration of osprey nests in Alberta — approximately fifteen. Artificial nesting platforms built on power poles have been placed in the water with the aid of a helicopter.

Other species found in the surrounding uplands include

Mule deer

wapiti, moose, mule deer, gray wolves and black bear.

This area is particularly attractive for boating, but care must be taken to avoid driftwood and snags just below the water's surface.

Osprey

Fish and Wildlife Division,
Drayton Valley 542-6767
Alberta Forestry Service,
Brazeau Ranger Station 894-3642

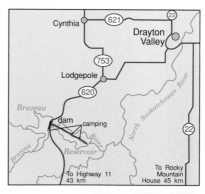

Cardinal River Divide

This height of land separates Arctic drainage (McLeod - Athabasca rivers) from drainage to Hudson's Bay (Cardinal - North Saskatchewan rivers). Patterned ground features and several rare plant species highlight the landscape. Tripoli Ridge, accessible from the top of the divide, is one of the few mountain areas along the eastern slope to have escaped the last glaciation, leaving a particularly rich alpine plant community.

Bighorn sheep, wapiti, moose, mule deer, grizzly bear, black bear and wolves are seen in this area. Hoary marmots are abundant and quite tame. Spruce grouse, blue grouse and Townsend's solitaires can be observed at higher elevations on the road through Mountain Park. Rosy finches, white-tailed ptarmigan, water pipits and horned larks are seen in the alpine zones of both watersheds. Many species of alpine flowers bloom in late July.

Cardinal River Divide

Hoary marmot

Wolf lichen

Road access past Whitehorse Creek may be restricted by snow between late October and late May.

Fish and Wildlife Division, Edson 723-8244
Fish and Wildlife Division, Hinton 865-8264

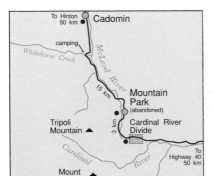

William A. Switzer Provincial Park

Streams connect five clear lakes and numerous wetlands through this broad valley of lodgepole pine, poplar and mature white spruce in the Rocky Mountain foothills. A day-long canoe trip from Jarvis Lake to Gregg Lake, through the heart of the 2,700-hectare park, may be the best way to see beavers, mink, muskrats and water birds, especially loons and grebes. The lakes and streams attract ospreys and bald eagles, and great gray owls live in the deciduous mixed-wood forests. In May, a chorus of common snipes, northern saw-whet owls and wood frogs can be heard at night, when you may also hear gray wolves.

Look for white-tailed and mule deer and the occasional wapiti and moose in the open meadows along Highway 40 from Hinton to Grande Cache. A mineral lick near the highway attracts ungulates so be cautious when driving through the park at dusk. North of the Berland River, Highway 40 leads through the winter range of mountain caribou.

Mushrooms (Gomphidius species)

Wood frog

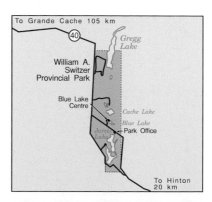

Provincial Parks Service,
Park Office 865-5600
Fish and Wildlife Division,
Hinton 865-8264

Caw Ridge

M. PYBUS

Caw Ridge

This alpine ridge is inhabited by one of the most diverse assemblies of large mammals in Alberta. Along with bighorn sheep, wapiti, mule deer, moose, white-tailed deer, grizzly bears, black bears and wolves, it includes one of the largest herds of mountain goats in the province.

Woodland caribou can be observed in spring and late fall as they migrate between summer and winter ranges. The hike up to the ridge from Beaverdam Creek leads along an old coal exploration trail bordered by lupines. Watch for ruffed, spruce and blue grouse.

The alpine environment above timberline includes forget-me-nots, moss campion and alpine cinquefoil, with a panorama of the Great Divide to the west and the boreal foothills to the east. Watch for horned larks, rosy finches and Townsend's solitaires.

Access to this site is challenging, requiring a four-wheel drive vehicle, but well worth the effort.

Bear tree (bark stripped for juice underneath)

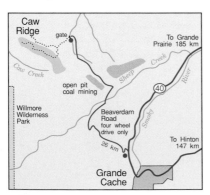

Fish and Wildlife Division,
Grande Cache 827-3356
Fish and Wildlife Division,
Edson 723-8244

Mountain goat

Bumble bee and crab spider

Englemann spruce branch

Viewing boardwalk at Cave and
Basin near Banff

Banff Townsite Area

Six species of orchid may be seen near the Marsh Trail at the Cave and Basin Hot Springs in spring and summer. Telescopes are provided to aid the search for aquatic mammals, yellowthroats, ruby-crowned kinglets, orange-crowned warblers, dark-eyed juncos and an abundance of waterfowl.

In late summer and fall, this is a major staging area for mallards, blue-winged and green-winged teals, lesser scaups and Barrow's goldeneyes. In January, watercress grows beside the snowbanks in microclimates warmed by thermal springs. American robins, killdeer, mallards, common goldeneyes and the occasional common snipe over-winter near the ice-free marsh.

Tropical fish species such as the mosquitofish, jewelfish and sailfin molly have been introduced and survive in the warm marsh water.

The self-guiding Fenland Nature Trail offers views of moose, deer and beaver along Forty Mile Creek. In the montane forest, listen for great horned, barred and pygmy owls at dusk.

At the wetlands along Vermilion Lakes Drive, look for beavers and muskrats as well as the bald eagles and osprey which nest nearby. The lakes are considered the most important single area in Banff for migrant waterfowl, including tundra and whistling swans and cinnamon teals.

Banff Townsite to Saskatchewan River Crossing
(via Bow Valley Parkway and Highway 93)

Km

0   Banff townsite. See preceding section. Drive west on Trans-Canada Highway and turn right onto Bow Valley Parkway (Highway 1A) at Kilometre 7.

8   Fireside Picnic area. Bighorn sheep are often seen here. The U-shaped Bow Valley, carved by glaciers, is sunnier, drier and more open on these south-facing slopes than on the other side of the river. The lodgepole pine forest frequently gives way to meadows, allowing a good view of wapiti, mule deer, coyote, bald eagle, and osprey. Note how much of the aspen along the parkway has been scarred by the large numbers of wapiti and deer which eat the bark during winter.

24 Johnston Canyon. A well-graded trail leads up a narrow gap cut by rushing, crystal waters. Black swifts, found in only a few places in Alberta, nest in the canyon walls. Other bird species include the American dipper, Clark's nutcracker, Townsend's solitaire, winter wren, Townsend's warbler, and the gray jay. The cool, moist environment supports a community of mosses, lichens and liverworts. Above Twin Falls, look for calypso orchids, asters, arnica and red paintbrush along the trail.

26 Willow swamp and moose meadows. This is a good place to see moose at dawn and dusk. Birds may include willow flycatcher, Brewer's blackbird and Lincoln's sparrow. Coyotes and wapiti frequent this area in winter — watch for tracks.

57 Lake Louise turnoff. Ascend to Lake Louise and Moraine Lake into the subalpine zone of Engelmann spruce and subalpine fir, paintbrush, white mountain avens, yellow columbine and alpine forget-me-not. The easy hike to Consolation Lake from Moraine Lake is a good way to escape the summer crowds and visit a tranquil subalpine lake under massive rock towers. Birds may include harlequin duck, American dipper, hermit and varied thrush, Clark's nutcracker and winter wren.

59 Icefields Parkway. This wilderness highway to Jasper in the shadow of the Great Divide follows the headwaters of three major river systems along the mountains of the Eastern Main Ranges. It crosses three ecological zones and offers splendid opportunities to see wildlife.

84-100 Mosquito Creek to Bow Summit. Grizzlies frequent this area.

99 Bow Summit. In this timberline zone, look for white mountain avens, globeflowers, western anemones and paintbrushes. A short trail provides insight into the transition from subalpine to alpine zones: the forest becomes islands of trees in protected areas, and those in the open become twisted, gnarled and dwarfed by fierce winds. On the ground, heathers begin to predominate. Look for least chipmunks, golden-mantled ground squirrels, pikas and marmots near the Peyto Lake viewpoint. Gray-crowned rosy finches and water pipits may also be seen.

116 Waterfowl Lakes. The lower lake features a popular campground. The less-visited upper lake contains many wet meadows along its edges, a good place to watch for moose. At the lakeside, look for juncos, common ravens and Barrow's goldeneyes. Wolves and woodland caribou may be seen in winter.

135 Saskatchewan River Crossing.

Saskatchewan River Crossing to Jasper Townsite
(via Icefields Parkway)

Km

0   Saskatchewan River Crossing. Proceed north. This road junction sits beneath the massifs of Mt. Wilson and Mt. Marcheson. Scan the grassy slopes of Mt. Wilson on the north and east side of the road. Bighorn sheep live on the lower slopes and mountain goats on the upper slopes and cliffs.

41 Parker Ridge. Here is one of the easiest trails in the mountain parks up to flower-filled alpine meadows. Ascend through feather mosses, heathers and grouseberry, where purple asters and arnica edge the trail, and listen for the *quick-three-beers* call of the olive-sided flycatcher. You soon enter the alpine zone which is starred with white mountain avens, alpine vetch, delicate blue alpine forget-me-nots, red and white heather and moss campion. Mountain goats may sometimes be seen on the west side of the ridge above the North Saskatchewan Glacier; listen for pikas in the rocks further up the ridge.

47 Wilcox Pass Trail. A relatively easy trail leads, in a few kilometres, to extensive alpine meadows that are home to an inquisitive flock of bighorn sheep. White-tailed ptarmigans nest in the pass.

51 Columbia Icefield. The Athabasca Glacier ends just above the main highway in a vast desolation of glacial rubble. A progression of plant communities is struggling to establish itself among the rocks where the glacier has retreated. In this succession, lichens are followed by cushion plants such as saxifrages, then by fireweed, purple vetch and small spruce and willows. Golden eagles hunt in the area. An interpretive centre is situated nearby.

61 Tangle Falls Viewpoint. Watch for bighorn sheep and Clark's nutcrackers.

68 - 76 Beauty Creek to Jonas Creek. Mountain caribou are regularly seen along here from November to April — watch for tracks and circular feeding craters. Grizzly bears may be sighted in May and June.

116 Look for the turnoff and viewpoint at a natural mineral lick used by mountain goats.

124 Athabasca Falls. The Athabasca River plunges 25 metres into a narrow gorge. Look for calypso orchids, red paintbrush, heart-leafed arnica and harebell near the trails.

124-151 Black bears frequent this section in May and June.

126   Horseshoe Lake. This quiet pond under the sandstone out-croppings of Mount Hardisty offers many ledges on which to sit while watching for Barrow's goldeneyes, ospreys, bald eagles, loons, grebes and moose.

151   Whistler's Campground. The surrounding forest is home to a large herd of wapiti which can be readily observed on the road side, especially in early morning and evening. September is a good time to hear the high-pitched whistling bugles of the bulls.

155   Jasper townsite. See next section.

Jasper Townsite Area

Wapiti and mule deer wander freely through commercial and residential areas of Jasper townsite, especially in spring, autumn and winter. At Cottonwood Slough, on Pyramid Lake Road, you might see common yellowthroats, Wilson's warblers, and northern waterthrushes, along with waterfowl such as the ring-necked duck, pied-billed grebe and sora. Moose may sometimes be seen at the slough as well, and on the road into Snaring Campground. The Old Fort Point Trail just south of the townsite leads up grassy ridges, a good grazing spot for bighorn sheep. Drive carefully: the sheep are frequently encountered right on Highway 16 near Disaster Point northeast of Jasper townsite, and near the road to Miette Hot Springs. Harlequin ducks and American dippers can be found at the Athabasca River near the town. Mountain caribou are occasionally seen on the Bald Hills above Maligne Lake, and American dippers and black swifts may be encountered at the lake itself. Gray wolves are attracted to the large numbers of deer and wapiti which winter near the townsite, and coyotes and ravens scavenge the remains of their kills.

Near the townsite, an aerial tramway whisks visitors 973 metres to the alpine heights of rounded Whistler's Summit. The open tundra of the summit ridge is frequented by white-tailed ptarmigan, horned larks, golden eagles, northern harriers, gray-crowned rosy finches, as well as marmots and golden-mantled squirrels. Wildflowers include white mountain avens, alpine buttercups, alpine harebell, moss campion, yellow paintbrush, arctic poppy, Lyall's saxifrage and western and alpine anemone.

Edmonton to Calgary (via Calgary Trail)

The divided highway between Edmonton and Calgary has a wide range of sighting opportunities along its 270-kilometre length. The roadside ditches, together with field margins of farmed areas, provide a major attraction to birds of prey on the lookout for small mammals, especially Richardson's ground squirrels. Snowy owls and short-eared owls are frequently sighted in winter and three species of hawk, the rough-legged (identified by its "boxer shorts"), the red-tailed (with a low belly band) and the Swainson's (with a bib beneath its chin) can be seen from spring to fall. Red-tailed and Swainson's hawks are most likely to be seen in summer. The accompanying illustrations are designed to provide positive identification, although the hawks may also be seen in darker phases than those pictured.

Rough-legged hawk

Km

0   City of Edmonton. Proceed south on Calgary Trail. Rock doves are prevalent among the higher buildings on the southern outskirts of the city.

8   Blackmud Creek shelters songbirds in the trees along its watercourse.

23   Leduc Pond, west of the Leduc turn-off, is home to a number of ducks, grebes and coots.

25-40   Occasional groves of sheltering aspen provide habitat for many songbirds. Mountain bluebirds are now sighted in the open areas, both here and further south along the highway. Bird nests can be seen in the aspen groves in winter.

46   Pipestone Creek crossing has marsh area on both sides of the highway.

90   The Battle River valley attracts a wide range of bird life to the mixed-wood habitat on both north and south slopes, and the willow marsh and open water along the river course. Ducks can

Swainson's hawk

often be spotted on the open water channels.

96   Morningside turn-off. The J.J. Collette Natural Area, a mosaic of forest, wetlands and meadow, is located 1.5 km south of Morningside. Great blue herons, red-winged blackbirds, ducks, gulls and terns are likely to be found on the ponds here. Wildflowers are plentiful in the meadows. Look for prairie crocuses, twin-flowers, marsh marigolds, violets and several orchid species. Songbirds are concentrated in the area as well.

113   Barnett Lake, surrounded by spruce and aspen, lies to the southeast of the highway, adjacent to College Heights. Water birds are usually found along the southern edge of the lake.

Red-tailed hawk

139   The valley of the Red Deer River shelters mature spruce-poplar forest. Here, the Red Deer River contains goldeye, northern pike, walleye and sauger fish species.

148   Slack Slough, visible on both sides of the highway south of Red Deer, provides ideal habitat for water birds. Swans can be seen in spring and fall to the east of the highway. Canada geese nest on the large bales deposited in the shallow waters.

155   Look to the west for the first sight of the Rocky Mountains.

195-210 Transition zone from parkland to prairie. Richardson's ground squirrels are regularly seen in spring and summer along the sides of the roadways.

Short-eared owl

270   Nose Hill with its native prairie grassland can be seen to the west across the valley. Updrafts along the bare hills to the north of Calgary give seemingly effortless flight to soaring raptors.

Continue south to the city of Calgary.

Snowy owl

*Moss campion
(following page)*

EGON BORK

89

The 50 most sought after wildlife species in Alberta and where to find them

* American white pelican   E S S F W

Large lakes of northern Alberta esp. Lac La Biche. Lakes in Cold Lake district.

Baird's sparrow   U S S F W

SE lush grasslands and grassy lake bottoms, esp. Gough and Sullivan Lakes, SE of Stettler.

Bald eagle   E S S F W

Northern lakes in summer. Rivers and mountains in migration.

Barred owl   R S S F W

Mature mixed wood forests near lakes, northern Alberta.

Barrow's goldeneye   E S S F W

Vermilion Lakes, Banff. Small lakes, Jasper.

Bighorn sheep   E S S F W

Along roads, any mountain N.P.

Black swift   E S S F W

Johnston Canyon, Banff N.P. Maligne Canyon, Jasper.

Black-backed woodpecker   U S S F W

Mature coniferous woods in winter. Recent forest fire areas.

Blackburnian warbler   R S S F W

Sir Winston Churchill P.P. Cold Lake P.P. (Good for other boreal wood warblers as well.) Police Point Park during migration.

Bohemian waxwing   E S S F W

Along Route 40 toward Grande Cache in summer. In cities of Edmonton, Red Deer, and Calgary in winter, with mountain ash trees.

Boreal owl   R S S F W

Northern Alberta. Foothills forests. Mature conifers.

Buff-breasted sandpiper   U S S F W

Shorebird migration Beaverhill Lake at Tofield.

* Burrowing owl   R S S F W

Local in SE grasslands, esp. between Hanna and Brooks.

Calliope hummingbird   R S S F W

Mountain parks, esp. townsite feeders in Waterton. Beaver ponds in Bow Valley P.P. Town of Seebe.

Canada lynx   U S S F W

Scarce along east slopes and northern forests. Wood Buffalo N.P.

Connecticut warbler   R S S F W

Whitney Lakes P.P., semi-open aspen woods.

Cougar   U S S F W

Waterton N.P. in winter. Vicinity of airport in Jasper townsite. Kananaskis country.

* Ferruginous hawk   E S S F W

Grasslands of SE Alberta, esp. vicinity of Hanna.

Fisher   U S S F W

Scarce in mountain parks and northern old-growth forests.

Golden eagle   E S S F W

Mountain parks. Southern prairie coulees.

Golden-crowned sparrow   R S S F W

Mountain parks. Tonquin Valley. Cardinal Divide near Mountain Park, SE of Hinton.

Gray wolf   R S S F W

Wolf howls occur in summer in Banff and Jasper N.P.s. Interpretive programs are available. Wood Buffalo N.P. near bison herds.

Great gray owl　　R S S F W

Northern Alberta in winter, esp. High Level. Also Caroline, Water Valley, and Hinton vicinity.

Grizzly bear　　R S S F W

Scan mountain slope across Cameron Lake, Waterton Lakes N.P., slopes above facility complex Saskatchewan Crossing, Banff N.P.

Harlequin duck　　E S S F W

Mountain rivers. Waterton River bridge at Waterton N.P., Bow River in Banff N.P.

Lark sparrow　　E S S F W

SE grasslands, esp. Dinosaur P.P. Badlands-sagebrush ecozone.

Long-billed curlew　　E S S F W

E grasslands, esp. between Brooks and Medicine Hat.

MacGillivray's warbler　　E S S F W

Mountain parks, especially along avalanche clearings. Valleys in Cypress Hills P.P.

Mountain goat　　E S S F W

Banff and Jasper N.P.s, esp. Disaster Point, Jasper.

Northern hawk-owl　　R S S F W

Black spruce bogs and winter roadsides, northern Alberta and the foothills. Best chance near High Level.

Northern pygmy-owl　　U S S F W

Mountains and eastern slopes. Imitate call.

* Peregrine falcon　　R S S F W

Sites of shorebird concentration during migration, esp. Beaverhill Lake. Downtown AGT buildings in Edmonton and Calgary.

Pileated woodpecker　　R S S F W

Mature wooded regions. Dry Island P.P., Lesser Slave Lake area.

* Piping plover　　R S S F W

Selected lakeshores in parkland region of east-central Alberta.

Prairie falcon　　E S S F W

Dinosaur P.P., badlands and river valleys through the prairies in summer. Foothills of Cardinal River Divide during migration.

Prairie rattlesnake　　R S S F W

Rock piles along Milk River and base of coulees.

Pronghorn　　E S S F W

SE Alberta. TransCanada Highway between Brooks and Medicine Hat.

Red-necked grebe　　E S S F W

Lakes and ponds east central Alberta, esp. Elk Island N.P.

Sage grouse　　R S S F W

Tours in spring from Medicine Hat. Contact Police Point Interpretive Centre. Highway 41 south of Cypress Hills.

Snowy owl　　R S S F W

Open fields, airports, and fence posts in winter.

Three-toed woodpecker　　R S S F W

Foothills and mountain park conifers. River valley in Red Deer and Edmonton. Crimson Lake P.P., Cochrane-Sundre area.

Townsend's solitaire　　R S S F W

Canyons and steep slopes in mountain parks. Along highway through Peter Lougheed P.P. Yamnuska Mountain near Bow Valley P.P.

* Trumpeter swan　　E S S F W

NW Alberta. Grande Prairie vicinity.

Varied thrush　　E S S F W

Cameron Lake, Waterton Lakes N.P.

Western grebe　　E S S F W

Larger lakes central and northern Alberta, esp. Lac La Biche and Cold Lake.

White-tailed ptarmigan　　R S S F W

Mt. Alpine. Most easily viewed from Whistler Mountain, Jasper.

* Whooping crane　　U S S F W

Nests only in Wood Buffalo N.P.

Wolverine　　U S S F W

Scarce in mountain parks backcountry. Mostly seen in Jasper and Waterton Lakes Park.

* Wood bison　　E S S F W

Wood Buffalo N.P. Captive herd in Elk Island N.P.

* Woodland caribou　　R S S F W

Hwy. 40 to Grande Cache and mountain ridges of Tonquin Valley (Jasper N.P.) in summer. Icefields Parkway in winter.

Jim Butler and Rob Stewart

Directory of Organizations

NATURAL HISTORY ORGANIZATIONS

National:

Canadian Nature Federation - Calgary Branch, 5127 Brisbois Drive, Calgary, AB T2L 2G3 (282-3997)

Canadian Nature Federation - Edmonton Branch, Box 8644, Station L, Edmonton, AB T6C 4J4

Canadian Parks and Wilderness Society (CPAWS) - Alberta Chapter, 11759 Groat Road, Groat Bldg., Edmonton, AB T5M 3K6 (453-8656)

Canadian Parks and Wilderness Society - Calgary/Banff Chapter, Box 608, Sub P.O. 91, University of Calgary, AB T2N 1N4 (232-0780)

Provincial:

Alberta Wilderness Association, Box 6398, Station D, Calgary, AB T2P 2E1 (283-2025)

Federation of Alberta Naturalists, Box 1472, Edmonton, AB T5J 2N5 (453-8629)

Maps Alberta, Alberta Forestry, Lands and Wildlife, 2nd flr. N. Tower, Petroleum Plaza, 9945-108 St., Edmonton, AB T5K 2C9 (427-3520)

Local:

Bow Valley Naturalists, Box 1693, Banff, AB T0L 0C0 (762-6320)

Buffalo Lake Naturalists, Box 1414, Stettler, AB T0C 2L0

Calgary Field Naturalists Society, Box 981, Calgary, AB T2P 2K4

Edmonton Bird Club, Box 4441, Edmonton, AB T6E 4T5

Edmonton Natural History Club, Box 1582, Edmonton, AB T5J 2N9

Lethbridge Naturalist Society, Box 1691, Lethbridge, AB T1J 4K4

Red Deer River Naturalists, Box 785, Red Deer, AB T4N 5H2

Trumpeter Swan Naturalists, R.R. 1, Wembley, AB T0H 3S0

Wagner Natural Area Society, 20 Forest Drive, St. Albert, AB T8N 1X2

Friends of Elk Island Society, R.R. 1, Site 4, Box 20, Ft. Saskatchewan, AB T8L 2N7

Waterton Natural History Association, Box 145, Waterton Lakes National Park, AB T0K 2M0

NATURE CENTRES / SANCTUARIES / OBSERVATORIES

Beaverhill Bird Observatory, Box 4943, Edmonton, AB T6E 5G3

Beaverhill Lake Nature Centre, Box 30, Tofield, AB T0B 4J0 (662-3191)

Clifford E. Lee Nature Sanctuary, R.R. 2, Site 6, Box 64, Winterburn, AB T0E 2N0

Ellis Bird Farm, P.O. Box 5502, Red Deer, AB T4N 6N1 (885-4200)

Helen Schuler Coulee Centre, City of Lethbridge Parks Department, Lethbridge, AB T1J 0P6 (320-3064)

Inglewood Bird Sanctuary, P.O. Box 2100, Postal Station M, Calgary, AB T2P 2M5 (269-6688 or 268-4718)

John Janzen Nature Centre, Box 2359, Edmonton, AB T5J 2R7 (428-7900)

Kerry Wood Nature Centre, 1, 6300-45 Ave., Red Deer, AB T4N 3M4 (346-2010)

Medicine River Wildlife Rehabilitation Centre, Box 115, Spruce View, AB T0M 1V0 (728-3467)

Ministik Hills Field Study Centre (located at Tofield, AB) 10554-83 Ave., Edmonton, AB T5J 2R7

Muskoseepi Park Interpretive Service, City of Grande Prairie, 9902-101 St., Grande Prairie, AB T8V 2P5 (538-0451 or 539-8000)

Police Point Interpretive Centre, City of Medicine Hat, 580-First Street SE, Medicine Hat, AB. T1A 8E6 (529-6225)

Shannon Terrace Environmental Education Centre, Box 2780, Calgary, AB T2P 0Y8 (297-7827)

Strathcona Wilderness Centre, Strathcona Recreation, Parks and Culture Department, 2025 Oak St., Sherwood Park, AB T8A 0W9 (922-3939)

GOVERNMENT ORGANIZATIONS
Federal:
Environment Canada - Western and Northern Region.

Canada Wildlife Service, 2nd flr, Twin Atria 2, 4999-98 Ave., Edmonton, AB T6B 2X3 (420-2525)

Parks Service, Western Regional Office, P.O. Box 2989, Stn. M, 220 4th Ave. SE, Calgary, AB T2P 3H8 (292-4401)

Provincial:
Alberta Fish and Wildlife, Department of Forestry Lands and Wildlife, Main Floor N. Tower, Petroleum Plaza, 9945-108 St., Edmonton, AB T5K 2G6 (427-6757)

Alberta Recreation and Parks, 16th Floor, Standard Life Bldg., 10405 Jasper Avenue, Edmonton, AB T5J 3N4 (427-9429)

Alberta Provincial Museum, 12845-102 Ave., Edmonton, AB (427-1786)

OTHER
Travel Alberta Information: in Alberta 222-6501, outside Alberta 1-800-661-8888

FURTHER READING

A Bird-finding Guide to Canada (1984) edited by J.C. Finlay, Hurtig Publishers Ltd., Edmonton

Birding: Jasper National Park (1988) by Kevin van Tighem and Andrew A. LeMessurier, Parks and People, Jasper

Finding Birds in Elk Island National Park (1988) by Judith Cornish, Friends of Elk Island Society, Fort Saskatchewan

A Nature Guide to Alberta (1980) edited by D.A.E. Spalding, Provincial Museum of Alberta, Publication No. 5, Hurtig Publishers and Alberta Culture, Edmonton

Parks in Alberta (1987) by Joy and Cam Finlay, Hurtig Publishers Ltd., Edmonton

Index

(Italics indicate photos and illustrations)

Alder, 67
Anemone, alpine, 87; Canada, 23; western, 85, 87
Arnica, 85, 86; heart-leaved, 87
Aster, 29, 85; purple, 86
Avens, white mountain, 85, 86, 87
Avocet, American, 26, 41, 61, *61*

Badger, 27, 32, 52, *32*
Bat, western small-footed, 53
Bear, 10, 45, 47, 57, 64, 68, 74, 77, 80, 82; grizzly, 5, 43, 73, 76, 85, 86, 94; black, 65, 73, 78, 79, 87
Beard-tongue, 46
Beaver, 10, 20, 22, 24, 27, 30, 31, 34, 37, 58, 60, 69, 71, 73, 81, 84, *20*
Beaverhill Natural Area, 18
Beehive Natural Area, 47
Beetle, long-horned, *59*
Big Sagebrush, 45
Birch, white, 57, 63, 67
Bison, plains, 5, 17, *17*; wood, 17, 66, 94
Bittern, American, 15, 52, 54, 58
Blackbird, Brewer's, 85; red-winged, 22, 41, 89, *20*; yellow-headed, 22, 29, 41, 59, 61, *59*
Bladderwort, 16
Blueberry, 65
Bluebird, mountain, 27, 56, 76, 88
Bobcat, 53
Bow Valley Provincial Park, 34
Brazeau Reservoir, 79
Brown-eyed Susan, 29
Buckbean, 25
Buffalo bean, 51
Buffalo Lake, 26
Buffaloberry, 19
Bufflehead, 23
Bulrushes, 23, 24
Bumble bee, *83*
Bunchberry, 67
Bunting, lark, 51; lazuli, 45, 53; snow, 56
Burnstick Lake, 24
Buttercup, alpine, 87
Butterwort, 16

Cactus, 30, 56; cushion, 38, *38*; prickly pear, 38, 40, 70, *70*
Campion, moss, *90*
Canvasback, 41
Cardinal River Divide, 80
Caribou, *77*; woodland, 5, 66, 77, 82, 85, 94; mountain, 81, 86, 87
Catbird, gray, 50
Cattail, 22, 71
Caw Ridge, 82
Chat, yellow-breasted, 56
Chickadee, 34; black-

capped, 22; boreal, 16, 22; mountain, 44, *44*
Chipmunk, 28, 65; least, 59, 73, 85; yellow-pine, 44
Cinquefoil, alpine, 82; marsh, 25; shrubby, 44
Clematis, blue, 22
Clifford E. Lee Nature Sanctuary, 15
Cold Lake Provincial Park, 62
Coltsfoot, 25
Columbine, yellow, 85
Coot, 22, 54, 88; American, 15, 19
Cormorant, double-crested, 17, 38, 41, 50, 52, 54, 60, 63, *54*
Cottontail, Nuttall's, 40, 49, 53
Cottonwood, 31, 36, 37, 40, 48, 49, 53, *49*
Cougar, 33, 43, 77, 93
Coyote, 5, 13, 14, 15, 20, 22, 26, 27, 31, 32, 33, 36, 52, 53, 58, 65, 69, 77, 84, 85, 87, *69*
Cranberry, highbush, 65, 67, 68
Crane, sandhill 25, 42, 65, 68, 74; whooping, 5, 59, 66, 94
Creeper, brown, 62
Crimson Lake Provincial Park, 25
Crocus, prairie, 29, 88
Cross Lake Provincial Park, 64
Crossbill, white-winged, 5, 44, 63, 73
Crowsnest Lake and River, 46
Curlew, long-billed, 38, 54, 56, 94
Cypress Hills Provincial Park, 50

Damselfly, *71*
Deer, 5, 13, 14, 15, 19, 22, 26, 27, 28, 31, 32, 37, 48, 49, 50, 64, 68, 71, 73, 74, 76, 77, 81, 82, 84, 87; mule, 4, 36, 43, 44, 45, 51, 53, 56, 79, 80, 84, 87, *79*; white-tailed, 20, 40, 41, 49, 58, 65, *26*
Devil's-club, 73
Dillberry Lake Provincial Park, 29
Dinosaur Provincial Park, 56
Dipper, American, 43, 76, 78, 85, 87
Dogwood, 19
Dove, mourning, 36, 37; rock, 88
Dry Island Buffalo Jump Provincial Park, 27
Duck, 18, 19, 22, 23, 24, 26, 27, 28, 29, 31, 32, 36, 46, 54, 58, 59, 61, 72, 89; harlequin, 33, 76, 85, 87, 94; ring-necked, 87; ruddy, 19; wood, 31
Duckweed, 71

Eagle, 10, 26, 30, 36, 37, 43, 66, 77, 78; bald, 18, 20, 31, 32, 64, 71, 72, 73, 76, 81,

84, 87, 93; golden, 27, 33, 45, 48, 49, 53, 56, 76, 86, 87, 93, *66*
East Porcupine Hills, 44
Egret, snowy, 52
Elk (see Wapiti)
Elk Island National Park, 17

Fairy bell, 22
Falcon, peregrine, 18, 66, 94; prairie, 27, 36, 48, 49, 53, 56, 94, *35*
Finch, gray-crowned rosy, 77, 85, 87; house, 46; rosy, 47, 80, 82
Fir, balsam, 63, 73; Douglas, 44, 46; subalpine, 85, *44*
Fireweed, 86
Fish Creek Provincial Park, 32
Fisher, 93
Flicker, northern, 34, 40, 59
Fly, crane, *26*
Flycatcher, 62; dusky, 50; Hammond's, 47; least, 16, 17, *16*; olive-sided, 22, 63, 86; willow, 85
Forget-me-not, alpine, 82, 85, 86
Fox, 13, 31; red, 5, 22, 49, 58
Frog, boreal chorus, 16, 19, *16*; spotted, 34, 46; wood, 16, 19, 34, 59, 81, *81*

Gaetz Lake Sanctuary, 22
Gentian, fringed, 15
Geranium, Bicknell's, 22; sticky, 44
Globeflower, 85
Godwit, marbled, 27, 38, 56, 61
Goldeneye, Barrow's, 17, 60, 84, 85, 87, 93; common, 23, 31, 79, 84
Goldeye, 27, 67, 74, 89
Goldfinch, American, 42
Goose, 28, 29, 32, 46, 54, 59; Canada, 5, 15, 18, 22, 23, 26, 31, 36, 38, 41, 54, 56, 58, 60, 65, 89, *41*; Ross', 26; snow, 18, 38, 41, *18*; greater white-fronted, 18, 38
Gooseberry Lake Provincial Park, 28
Gopher, northern pocket, 40, 42
Goshawk, northern, 16, 18, 68, 72
Grasshopper, *40*
Grayling, arctic, 5
Grebe, 5, 19, 22, 24, 46, 54, 72, 81, 87, 88; eared, 23, 61; horned, 61; pied-billed, 59, 87; red-necked, 15, 17, 20, 94, *17*; western, 20, 94
Grosbeak, evening, 64; pine, 64; rose-breasted, 19
Ground squirrel, 44; columbian, 33, 42, 45; Franklin's, 63; golden-mantled, 45, 77, 85, 87; Richardson's, 42, 58, 88, 89, *54*; thirteen-lined, 28, 29, 33, *29*
Grouse, blue, 42, 45, 76, 80, 82; ruffed, 15, 24, 26, 58, 64, 73, 82, *24*; sage, 94; sharp-tailed, 70; spruce, 24, 44, 80, 82

Grouseberry, 44, 86
Gull, 20, 28, 72, 89; California, 19, 41, 43, 54, 60, 63; Franklin's, 61; ring-billed, 19, 26, 41, 54, 60

Hare, snowshoe, 14, 15, 28, 44, 64, 65, 69, 73, *62*
Harebell, alpine, 87
Harrier, northern, 18, 23, 58, 87
Hawk, 5, 10, 26, 30; broad-winged, 15; ferruginous, 37, 56, 93; red-tailed, 18, 23, 32, 36, 37, 44, 58, 88, *58*; rough-legged, 18, 36, 88; Swainson's, 27, 31, 32, 37, 56, 88
Heather, 76, 85, 86, *76*
Helen Schuler Coulee Centre, 40
Heron, 10, 20, 29, 57; black-crowned night-, 17, 26, 41, 52, 60; great blue, 17, 24, 26, 27, 28, 42, 56, 58, 59, 60, 64, 65, 79, 89, *24*
Honeysuckle, 67
Hummingbird, calliope, 34, 43, 45, 93; rufous, 34, 43

Ibis, white-faced, 52
Inglewood Bird Sanctuary, 31

Jack rabbit, white-tailed, 27, 51, 53, *52*
Jay, gray, 20, 85; Steller's, 76
Jessie Lake, 61
Jewelfish, 84
Junco, dark-eyed, 16, 50, 84
Juniper, ground, 42, 44, 51

Kestrel, American, 49, 70, 78
Killdeer, 84
Kimiwan Lake, 72
Kingbird, eastern, 36, 37, 56; western, 56
Kingfisher, belted, 14, 20, 27, 37, 56, *37*
Kinglet, golden-crowned, 62; ruby-crowned, 14, 16, 84
Kleskun Hill Natural Area, 70
Krummholz, 75

Lady's-slipper, 16; Franklin's, 50; yellow, 15, 22, 34, *22*
Lake Newell, 54
Lamprey, northern, 67
Larch, alpine, *46*
Lark, horned, 51, 56, 77, 80, 82, 87
Lemming, northern bog, 25
Lesser Slave Lake Provincial Park, 73
Lichen, wolf, *80*
Lichens: lecanora, *45*; peltigera, *74*; xanthoria, *45*
Lily, glacier, 76; mariposa, 45; sand, *51*; western wood, 29, 34, *29*
Lily-of-the-valley, 15, 22
Lizard, short-horned, 51, *51*
Longspur, chestnut-collared, 54
Loon, common, 5, 20, 24, 46, 81, 87
Lynx, Canada, 5, 73, 93

McGregor Lake, 38
McKinnon Flats, 36
Mallard, 20, 23, 31, 62, 84, *36*
Marmot, 85, 87; hoary, 77, 80, *80*; yellow-bellied, 53
Marsh marigold, 25, 88
Marten, 47, 73
Meadowlark, western, 29, 51
Meadow rue, 44
Merganser, common, 31; hooded, 20, 60
Merlin, 14, 18, 72, 78
Mink, 24, 58, 59, 60, 62, 73, 81, *60*
Miquelon Lake Provincial Park, 19
Molly, sailfin, 84
Monkey-flower, red, 46; yellow, 46
Moose, 10, 17, 19, 20, 24, 45, 47, 48, 50, 57, 64, 66, 68, 71, 73, 74, 76, 77, 79, 80, 81, 82, 84, 85, 87, *74*
Mosquitofish, 84
Moth, polyphemus, *36*
Mountain goat, 10, 34, 76, 77, 82, 86, 94, *83*
Mouse, deer, 28, 40
Muskrat, 15, 20, 22, 24, 27, 30, 31, 37, 58, 59, 60, 69, 71, 73, 81, 84, *15*

Nighthawk, common, 53
Notikewin Provincial Park, 74
Nutcracker, Clark's, 45, 47, 76, 85, 86, *45*
Nuthatch, red-breasted, 22, 44

Orchid, 5, 22, 25, 34, 43, 50, 84, 89; Bog adder's-mouth, 16; calypso, 67, 85, 87, *25*; northern green bog, 16; sparrow's egg, 16
Oriole, northern, 14, 19, 24, 26, 36, 56
Osprey, 20, 43, 57, 64, 76, 79, 81, 84, 87, *79*
Ostrich fern, 74
Otter, river, 5
Outpost Wetlands Natural Area, 42
Ovenbird, 19, 50
Owl, barred, 63, 84, 93; boreal, 25, 63, 93; burrowing, 54, 93; great gray, 5, 20, 71, 81, 94; great horned, 5, 16, 17, 26, 31, 32, 40, 53, 56, 65, 71, 73, 84, *31*; northern hawk, 94; northern pygmy, 25, 84, 94; northern saw-whet, 14, 16, 17, 63, 70, 81, *14*, *70*; short-eared, 26, 58, 88; snowy, 88, 94

Paintbrush, 85; Indian, 76, *43*; red, 85, 87; yellow, 87
Pakowki Lake, 52
Partridge, gray, 31, 41, *41*
Pelican, American white, 5, 20, 26, 28, 36, 37, 38, 54, 57, 60, 63, 67, 73, 93, *38*, *67*
Perch, 24; yellow, 20, 59
Peter Lougheed Provincial Park, 76
Pewee, western wood, 19, 26

Phalarope, red-necked, 28
Pheasant, cock, 14; ring-necked, 31, 41
Phoebe, Say's, 56
Pika, 45, 75, 76, 77, 85, 86, *76*
Pike, 24, 74; northern, 20, 59, 64, 67, 79, 89, *67*
Pine, 15, 45, 64, 78; jack, 57, 59, 74; limber, 39, 44, *34*; lodgepole, 25, 34, 45, 46, 47, 74, 75, 81, 84
Pipit, Sprague's, 29, 58; water, 5, 77, 80, 85
Pincherry, 19
Pintail, northern, 41, *72*
Plover, piping, 26, 94
Police Point Park, 49
Poorwill, common, 50
Poplar, 13, 24, 28, 30, 45, 57, 63, 64, 81, 89; aspen, 5, 15, 17, 19, 23, 25, 26, 29, 32, 34, 42, 46, 58, 59, 61, 65, 68, 69, 84, 88, *28*; balsam, 19, 37, 67, 74
Poplar Creek, 65
Porcupine, 20, 40, 49, 52, 53, 58, *40*
Primrose, butte, 40; evening, 15, 22, 51
Pronghorn, 5, 48, 50, 51, 52, 54, 56, 94, *50*
Ptarmigan, white-tailed, 47, 75, 76, 77, 80, 86, 87, 94, *76*

Rail, 20, 54
Ram Falls Recreation Area, 78
Raspberry, wild, 19, 65, 67
Raven, common, 20, 79, 85, 87
Red Rock Coulee Natural Area, 51
Redpoll, common, 56, 64
Redstart, American, 50
Robin, American, 84
Rose, prickly, *28*; wild, 19, 65, 67, *65*
Rush Lake, 41

Sagebrush, 51
Salamander, long-toed, 34, 46, *46*; tiger, 34, *34*
Sandpiper, 20, 25, 72; buff-breasted, 93; spotted, 14
Sapsucker, red-naped, 46
Saskatoons, 19, 65, 69, *19*
Saskatoon Island Provincial Park, 69
Sauger, 89
Saxifrage, 86; Lyall's, 87
Scaup, lesser, 84
Scorpion, 51
Scoter, white-winged, 50
Sheep River Wildlife Sanctuary, 33
Sheep, bighorn, 5, 30, 33, 34, 43, 45, 46, 47, 75, 76, 77, 78, 80, 82, 84, 86, 87, 93, *33*
Shooting star, 23, *23*
Shoveler, northern, 38
Shrew, pygmy, 25; water, 25
Siffleur Wilderness Area, 77
Sir Winston Churchill Provincial Park, 63
Siskin, pine, 44
Skipper, Delaware, 53
Skunk, striped, 52

Slack Slough, 23
Slave River - Mountain Rapids, 67
Snake, bull, 53, 56; plains garter, 19, 52, *19*; prairie rattle, 51, 56, 94; red-sided garter, 19; western rattle, 53
Snipe, common, 41, 42, 59, 81, 84, *42*
Solitaire, Townsend's, 45, 47, 80, 82, 85, 94
Sora, 19, 62, 87
Sparrow, 37, 62; Baird's, 93; grasshopper, 51; lark, 29, 94; Le Conte's, 61; golden-crowned, 93; Lincoln's, 85; savannah, 58, 61; song, 17; swamp, 59; white-throated, 22, 64; vesper, 42, 58
Spider, black widow, 54; crab, 83
Spring beauty, western, *47*
Spruce, 17, 32, 47, 57, 64, 68, 78, 86, 89; black, 16, 25, 63, 65; Engelmann, 85; white, 34, 63, 65, 67, 74, 75, 81, *65*, *83*
Squirrel, red, 28, 64, 65, 73, 78, *78*
Stilt, black-necked, 52
Sucker, longnose, 64, *64*; white, 64
Sundew, 16, 25
Swallow, cliff, 43, 49, *27*; tree, 18, 36, 37, 79; violet-green, 43
Swallowtail, tiger, 53, *52*
Swan, 28, 29, 46, 89; trumpeter, 69, 94, *69*; tundra, 18, 23, 41, 69, 84; whistling, 84
Swift, black, 85, 87, 93

Tamarack, 25
Tanager, western, 25, 62
Teal, 62; blue-winged, 38, 84; cinnamon, 42, 52, 72, 84; green-winged, 19, 38, 84
Tern, 20, 89; black, 70; common, 26
Therien Lakes, 60
Thimbleberry, 44
Thrasher, brown, 37, 56, *37*
Thrush, 62; gray-cheeked, 70; hermit, 29, 43, 63, 85; northern water, 42, 87; Swainson's, 43, 63, 70; varied, 43, 45, 76, 85, 94
Toad, 63; boreal, 34, 46; plains spadefoot, 5, 56; western, 16
Towhee, rufous-sided, 53, 56
Trout, 39, 41, 47; brown, 36, 46; bull, 46; cutthroat, 46, 78; lake, 62; rainbow, 46
Turkey vulture, 27
Turkey, wild, 50
Turnstone, ruddy, 59
Turtle, painted, 40
Twin-flower, 89, *73*
Tyrrell Lake, 41

Umbrella-plant, 46

Valerian, 76
Vermilion Provincial Park, 58
Vetch, alpine, 86; purple milk, 23, 86
Violet, 23, 89
Vireo, red-eyed, 17; solitary, 62
Vole, meadow, 40

Wabamun Lake, 20
Wagner Natural Area, 16
Walleye, 20, 59, 62, 74, 89
Wapiti (Elk), 5, 10, 17, 44, 47, 48, 50, 74, 76, 77, 79, 80, 81, 82, 84, 85, 87
Warbler, 5, 27, 31, 47, 49, 59, 62, 64, 71, 73; bay-breasted, 62, 63; black-throated green, 63; black-burnian, 62, 63, 93, *63*; Cape May, 62, 63; Connecticut, 59, 93; MacGillivray's, 43, 50, 94; magnolia, 63; mourning, 63; orange-crowned, 50, 84; palm, 59, 63; Tennessee, 59; Townsend's, 47, 85; Wilson's; yellow, 19; yellow-rumped, 16
Waterton Lakes National Park, 43
Waxwing, bohemian, 14, 93; cedar, 64
Weasel, long-tailed, 31, 69
White Goat Wilderness Area, 77
Whitefish, 67; lake, 20, 38; mountain, 46
Whitemud Creek Ravine, 14
Whitney Lakes Provincial Park, 59
Wigeon, Eurasian, 52
Willet, 27, 61
William A. Switzer Provincial Park, 81
Willow, 16, 22, 36, 59, 67, 85, 86
Winagami Lake, 72
Wintergreen, 15
Wolf, gray (timber), 5, 66, 73, 77, 79, 80, 81, 82, 85, 87, 93
Wolverine, 43, 77, 94
Wood Buffalo National Park, 66

Wood Nymph, common, *42*

Woodchuck, 69
Woodpecker, black-backed, 93; downy, *22*; hairy, 50; pileated, 14, 16, 22, 94; three-toed, 22, 34, 94
Wren, marsh, 29, 52; rock, 51, 53, 56, *55*; winter, 85
Writing-On-Stone Provincial Park, 53
Wyndham-Carseland Provincial Park, 37

Yamnuska Mountain, 34
Yellowlegs, greater, 25, 61; lesser, 28, 61
Yellowthroat, common, 84, 87
Young's Point Provincial Park, 71